8

JUAN MANUEL FANGIO

JUAN MANUEL FANGIO

MOTOR RACING'S GRAND MASTER

LUD VIG SEN KARL LUDVIGSEN

Foreword by Karl Kling

Featuring the photography of Rodolfo Mailander

Haynes Publishing

In memory of

Stefan Habsburg-Lothringen

Creative engineer, educator and friend
in the Fangio years and beyond.

First published in September 1999

British Library Cataloguing in Publication Data:
A catalogue record for this book is available from the British Library

ISBN 1 85960 625 3

Library of Congress catalog card no 99-72052

Haynes North America Inc.,
861 Lawrence Drive, Newbury Park, California 91320, USA.

Published by Haynes Publishing,
Sparkford, Nr Yeovil, Somerset BA22 7JJ.

Tel: 01963 440635 Fax: 01963 440001
Int.tel: +44 1963 440635 Int fax: +44 1963 440001

E-mail: sales@haynes-manuals.co.uk
Web site: http://www.haynes.com

Designed and typeset by G&M, Raunds, Northamptonshire
Printed and bound in Great Britain by J.H. Haynes & Co. Ltd

Jacket illustrations

Front cover: Early in his final championship season, 1957, Juan Fangio puts the V12-engined 250F Maserati through its paces at Monte Carlo during practice for the Grand Prix. (The Klementaski Collection)

Back cover: Juan Fangio elects to drive solo in the 1955 Mille Miglia. In spite of losing fuel injection to one of the eight cylinders of his Mercedes-Benz 300SLR, he places second to Stirling Moss and Denis Jenkinson in a similar car. (Bradshaw from LaFollette Collection)

Frontispiece

Captured in 1955 by Bernard Cahier, the open, frank and friendly gaze of Juan Manuel Fangio bespeaks his personality: calm, conservative, sincere and always willing to learn – great attributes for a racing driver.

Contents

Introduction

How shall we measure the man? Shall we count up his 24 victories in the 51 qualifying Grand Prix races he entered in the first nine years of the world drivers' championship? Shall we remind ourselves that he sat on pole in more than half of those races, 28 to be exact? And that only four other racing drivers – none still competing – have more poles to their credit? And that he set fastest lap in 23 of his championship Grands Prix? Of those still driving only Michael Schumacher has topped that total.

Juan Manuel Fangio took part in some 200 automobile races. The total would be much higher if you counted – as some do – the individual timed stages of the great South America open-road contests. Two hundred is not a massive total; Stirling Moss competed in more than twice as many. But Fangio aimed to drive the great cars in the great races and in this he succeeded admirably. Of those 200 races he won 78 and was placed in 69 more.

Yet it is with Formula 1 racing that Fangio is especially and indelibly associated. 'It is true that I always preferred Formula 1,' he said. 'That was just a little bit because I liked to sit in the middle of the car. Then you achieve a consistent view to each side from which you can judge placing of the car in corners both to left and right.' By winning the world drivers' championship in five of his eight full Formula 1 seasons he put down a marker that no other driver has yet approached.

One who might have, Ayrton Senna, admired Fangio as a man as well: 'What he did in his time is something that was an example of professionalism, of courage, of style and as a man, a human being. Every year, there is a winner of the championship but not necessarily a world champion. I think Fangio is the example of a true world champion.'

British fans, voting in 1998 for the best-ever Formula 1 driver 40 years after Juan Manuel last raced, agreed with Senna. They ranked Fangio first ahead of Jim Clark and Senna himself. In his lifetime Fangio was showered with awards from Germany, Italy, France and Argentina, where he was granted an honorary professorship. These he received with the grace, humility and modesty that characterised all his years.

'Victory is satisfying, none can deny it,' he told his biographer Roberto Carozzo. 'However, after the garlands and the cheering crowds it is a relief to get away and forget all about motor racing. The day afterwards it all comes back, and you relive the race lap by lap, feeling thankful that you did your best and it was good enough.'

I also like another Fangio comment to Carozzo: 'Those who are too brave never make history because they don't know why they have won when they win. A really good driver should always know why he has won and why he has lost.'

Roberto Carozzo's is the last, deepest and most personal book about Juan Fangio. I am fond of the first such book by Federico Kirbus and Ronald Hansen; my friend and colleague Kirbus was the intermediary for my personally autographed Fangio photo. Other books about Fangio have been written by Günther Molter, Olivier Merlin, Stirling Moss with Doug Nye, and by Fangio in co-operation with his manager Marcello Giambertone.

Denis Jenkinson's book about the film *Fangio* has much to say. Of the film itself I am not so fond, although I am grateful to Chris Nixon for loaning it to me. I am grateful to these and the many other sources referenced in the Bibliography, especially the *Auto Racing Analysis* of Fangio's career compiled by Steve Schuler.

A special pleasure in researching the life of Juan Fangio was rediscovering the snappy, evocative and stylish prose of Rodney Walkerley, sports editor of *The Motor* who wrote as 'Grande Vitesse'. If you find him quoted often it's because he brings the man and his races to vivid life.

I wish to express my gratitude to Paul Parker for editorial and research assistance, to Paola Arrighi and Maria Arizmendi, who helped me with interviews and translations, and most especially to Karl Kling for his open and great-hearted Foreword. Meeting and talking with Kling has been an honour and a pleasure. I am deeply indebted to my wife Annette for her encouragement of this project and to everyone at Haynes as well.

Luis Barragán and Alfredo Safe of the Fundacion Museo J. M. Fangio in Balcarce provided valuable help. Magnificent assistance was rendered by Stanislav Peschel and Gerd Langer of the Daimler-Benz Classic Archive, Ermanno Cozza of Maserati and Riccardo Andreoni of Ferrari in providing photos and documentation. Donald Davidson helped with information on Fangio's visit to Indy in 1958.

Among the photos from our archives those of Rodolfo Mailander stand out; without them this book would not have been possible. Peter Keen's are superb as well. Other photographers well represented are Bernard Cahier, Louis Klementaski and Guy Griffiths. Many thanks to them all.

I took a snap or two myself in March 1954 when Fangio and Castellotti came to Thompson, Connecticut, of all places, to demonstrate a Maserati and a Siata for importer Tony Pompeo. My Spanish-speaking friend Stefan Habsburg introduced me to Fangio and helped me get his autograph.

Several years later in New York I was on hand, with a lady friend, when Fangio was present for the start of a rally. A comely blonde, she told me afterward that she'd been a weak-kneed recipient of that blue-eyed Fangio gaze that won so many female conquests. His vision was excellent both on and off the track.

I would like to give his protégé Juan Manuel Bordeu a few final words before I let Juan Manuel's career speak for itself:

'Through Fangio I got a very striking insight into the human side of motor racing. I understood the natural gifts he had that enabled him to win. That tenacity, that pride, his physical toughness, his tremendous faith in himself. The wonderful thing about him is that this tenacity and will to win never blinded him or made him forget that motor racing has a human side.

'He was so superior. I saw the difference between a good driver and a genius. He was a genius, a natural. He was not reserved about telling others how he did what he did. They just had to do it after he had done it.'

Karl Ludvigsen
Islington, London
March 1999

Foreword

by Karl Kling

German 2-litre sports car champion 1947–49 and Mercedes-Benz team driver 1951–55

When the name Fangio is mentioned, for me he was one of the greatest drivers of those days, and one of the most congenial and fair! A good colleague and a principled sportsman. Few were quite so fair as Fangio. I was in a position to experience that. Few were as open and above-board as Fangio was at that time.

In Argentina Juan Perón himself was a fan of motor sports. He provided a great deal of support for Fangio. After he took note of him in the beginning (Fangio had his own private Grand Premio Standard Chevrolet, which is what made him great in the first place) Perón recognised very early on that Fangio was a great talent, and supported him.

I came into contact with Fangio fairly frequently in the sport. Once, for example, I was faster than him at the Nürburgring. Fangio immediately moved aside. He didn't defend his position or anything like that. Twice at Monza I was faster than him at certain places – and he moved over. I can't say the same of many others.

Fangio remarked: 'We came up against each other a few times.' Perhaps at such moments I had a bit better engine; that could well be. Purely from a driving standpoint he was better, that's all there was to it. That's why I won't hear a word said against him. That's why I'm honest about him.

Many opportunities came my way. Sometimes I had a slightly better engine; engine performance was scattered over a broader range then. They were not all the same. When I got into the car I could tell immediately: 'You've got a good engine' or 'You've got a bad engine.'

Fangio didn't notice this. Because Fangio was actually not all that well versed technically. He sat in the car and was satisfied with it. He never said, 'I'd prefer different shock absorbers for this course, or a different gear ratio.' Fangio got in the car and drove it.

However, Fangio was the faster. He could always pull out a few more stops. From time to time it was stated accurately enough that he could powerslide. Earlier this had always been his objective.

I'm not a powersliding driver, nor am I an advocate of such techniques. I think that a clean, smooth lap brings me better results. But Fangio – at the extremity – could control a powerslide that was colossal. And he mastered it right to the ultimate limit.

Personally as a driver I profited a great deal from him. Frequently I found myself driving behind him; when that happened I watched his technique. I wanted to learn something from him. It was a unique experience – and rarely hazardous.

I can state quite confidently that Fangio and I were close friends. There is scarcely a driver – and I know a great many – whom I learned to esteem more than Juan Manuel Fangio. Also as a friend and comrade.

Juan Fangio and Karl Kling first team up to race for Mercedes-Benz in 1951. They are team-mates again in 1953 at Alfa Romeo and in 1954–55 at Mercedes-Benz, whose photographers took these snaps of two men whose mutual respect and friendship were born of long experience. Kling was the elder by less than a year.

Ford
SOMBREROS

CHAPTER 1

Argentine glories

We've all heard the legend. Somewhere far away, in an obscure region like Patagonia, there's a truck driver who would be the world's fastest and best Grand Prix racer if he only had the chance. Instead he slogs away on those dusty roads, little knowing or even dreaming that he has the skills that could take him to the top of the world of motorsports. Funny thing – the legend turned out to be true!

It wasn't quite true, of course. Juan Manuel Fangio realised he had petrol in his veins as soon as he was aware there were such things as cars. 'As far back as I can remember,' he said, 'I was fascinated by everything that rolled on four wheels. The feeling dominated my childhood.' And he was keen on driving, and driving fast. Yet the idea of winning races, and indeed of winning with Formula 1 cars, was far from his mind. One simply did not think of such things. 'When I started racing,' Fangio told his biographer Roberto Carozzo, 'I had no thought of becoming a famous driver. Every time victory was achieved it came as a complete surprise.'

Gilberto Bianculli rides shotgun for Fangio in the races in 1938 and '39 in the Ford V8-powered Special in which Juan, at 26, first satisfies himself that he has the makings of a successful racing driver.

Remote though Argentina was from the European nexus of Grand Prix racing, young Fangio did not lack for role models in his native land. A Buenos Aires horse-racing track had been the venue for Argentina's first auto race in 1901. In 1910 the first town-to-town race was held from Buenos Aires to Cordoba almost 500 miles away, setting a pattern for long-distance over-the-road races in Argentina that would endure for half a century.

Circuit racing continued as well, for example the 500 miles of Rafaela over 5.4 miles of unmade roads in Santa Fe province. Raul Riganti, one of the great Argentine racing names, was Rafaela's first winner in 1926. Riganti was the first Argentine sportsman to race seriously abroad, competing in the Indianapolis 500 in 1923 (Bugatti), 1933 (Chrysler) and 1940 (Maserati). Expatriate Englishman Eric Forrest Greene won at Rafaela in 1928. An immigrant from Galicia, Spain, Carlos (born Karel) Zatuszek won the Rafaela 500-mile race in 1935 in a Mercedes-Benz SSK during an astonishingly successful career that ended in a fatal crash in 1937.

Drivers like these became role models for a man born on 24 June 1911, the feast day of San Juan, to a family living in modest circumstances in Balcarce, a town of 40,000 for whom potato farming was a vocation they were glad to have. Arriving fourth in a family that would ultimately count six offspring, Juan Manuel Fangio received his surname from his father Loreto.

Loreto Fangio had been only seven when he arrived in Argentina in 1887 with his father Giuseppe from Italy, where he was born in Castiglione Messer Marino in the mountainous Abruzzi. Dozens of Fangios live there still. Little Loreto had scarcely tasted meat before coming to South America. In the Abruzzi it was Italian maize porridge: 'polenta, always polenta.' When he was 19, in 1903, Loreto Fangio married Herminia Deramos, born in Argentine Tres Arroyos of Italian parents. His skills as a stonemason, plasterer and painter were valued in a growing town 220 miles south of the hub of Argentina, Buenos Aires.

Cars and trucks soon became vital to Argentina's sprawling infrastructure, which depended on her ability to move products from farm to market. The Americans were the first to meet that demand with their robust though crude autos. They did so with plants set up in Argentina, as required by its laws, to assemble cars and trucks there. By 1924 Ford's Buenos Aires branch could assemble 45,000 vehicles a year. Fords and Chevrolets were Argentina's staple autos, although other makes filtered in in smaller numbers.

The farther one was from Buenos Aires the more essential it was to have the skills locally to repair this hard-worked rolling stock without recourse to fresh parts or shop manuals. 'You had to be a bit of a blacksmith as well as a mechanic,' Fangio recalled. 'You couldn't easily get spares as you can today.' Appropriately enough his first apprenticeship, at the age of 11, was with Balcarce smithy Francisco Cerri. Juan continued his studies there, then in the car-repair workshops of Capettini, Carlini and the Estévez Ford agency.

'I began by cleaning parts, as all apprentices do,' he recalled. 'Later I learned to do the odd job by looking at how others did it. That was what apprenticeship was all about in those days – looking on and "stealing" knowledge from those who knew more.' Young Fangio's skills were given their final polish at Balcarce's Studebaker agency, run by Miguel Vigiano. Files and stones were his tools, not machines, as he learned to repair, rebuild and make from scratch to a standard that made him the workshop's top fitter.

Driving lessons came at no charge at Vigiano's, said Roberto Carozzo: 'He was trusted to deliver and collect customers' cars from Buenos Aires, driving across dirt roads that turned to mud when it rained. An animated talker, he illustrates the problem of getting a car out of deep mud, slapping his hands together, beating his thighs, mimicking the crunch of gears and the sound of wheels screaming. He says he learned valuable lessons about driving: use the gearbox to slow down, keep the car balanced and the wheels evenly loaded.'

For the first 50 years of his life Fangio drove without a licence: 'I only got a licence to drive on public roads in 1961, for a journey I had to make to Brazil. Till then I had never had a driving licence, as when I learned to drive out there in the country, nobody had one. People simply learned to drive and off they went.'

Speaking of driving, the special appeal of the Studebaker agency was that Miguel Vigiano raced cars and in his workshop prepared modified touring cars for racing. This was a bacillus to which Juan Fangio was as vulnerable as the pleurisy that laid him low for months in 1927. And when Vigiano paid him with an Overland auto in lieu of salary, Fangio immediately set about making it into a racing car. 'I already felt I was a racer,' he reflected later.

But another decade would pass before Juan really raced. In the meantime he and his friends raised a bit of hell. 'We went out on the road and pretended to have run out of petrol, so that we could get a full tank,' he told Carozzo. 'We would flag down cars and tell them that we'd run out. When they said they were sorry that they had no hose for siphoning from one tank to another, we told them not to worry and that we had one. What we had in our car was not a little hose but a great big one. Petrol would flow from one tank to another like nobody's business. These little pranks can degenerate into something else, however, as the "dare" has to get greater and greater. It can lead to adventures in which no one wants to look yellow. It is then that things may take a bad turn.'

The boy grew into a man during his year of military service in 1932. 'Before being in the army I was a rebel, I didn't respect a thing,' he admitted. 'But when I left I began to respect people, and to understand that others had as many rights as I had. Before going into the army one thinks that one is a god. In the army you realised that you were nothing more than a number, a small cog.'

On 25 October 1936 Juan first tried his skill as a driver in a minor race at Benito Juárez: 'I remember the car was a Ford taxi! It was borrowed from a friend, and we took the body off. After the race we put the bodywork back on, and it was then used as a taxi again.' He raced under the name 'Rivadavia', a Patagonian seaside town. 'I chose "Rivadavia" because it's the name of the football club I played for in Balcarce,' he said. 'My friends were in it too. I put myself down as Rivadavia almost as a way of taking them along with me on this first experience of racing. They'd given me so much encouragement in getting the car ready.' Partnered by Gilberto Bianculli, whose father had provided the Model A taxi, they had to retire when a bearing seized after a loss of oil.

Fangio was a capable mid-field player for Rivadavia and other clubs, attracting offers from the nearby resort town of Mar del Plata. He was held in high esteem not only for his skills on the field but also for his ability to drive and repair the team's transport. His characteristic stance on the pitch earned him the nickname that would follow him throughout his lifetime: *'el Chueco'* – 'the bandy-legged one'. The later Fangio legend would attribute this to bow legs earned as a gaucho on the Pampas, but Juan Manuel much preferred horsepower of the four-wheeled ilk.

Rivadavia's players took charge when they heard that Fangio and a friend might be lured by the bright lights of Mar del Plata. Fearful of losing star footballers and a great mechanic, they encouraged Juan to set up a car workshop of his own in Balcarce. 'My footballing friends were the starting point and foundation of everything,' he said. They helped build Fangio's first workshop on his father's land and later backed his move to a better site only a block from the town's central square. Soon he did well enough to set up a YPF petrol station on the corner opposite the workshop.

Although a naturally wealthy nation, Argentina suffered with the developed world in the Great Depression. Juan Fangio and his partners had to work doubly hard in the 1930s to develop their business. His dream of racing now nestled in a niche in his memory. But might racing not be a way to promote Fangio, Duffard & Co? This idea was encouraged by Juan's younger brother Ruben Renato Fangio, better known as 'Toto', who had joined the firm. On his recommendation they bought a racer with a known pedigree, a stripped-down 1934 Ford with an 80-horsepower V8 engine, and entered it for the races on a 4-mile paved road circuit at Necochea on 27 March 1938.

There the little Ford was up against heavy metal: Carlos Arzani's 3.8-litre Grand Prix Alfa Romeo, Fermin Martin in the late Carlos Zatuszek's SSK and an Indianapolis Chrysler. But Fangio qualified in the front row for the first heat and briefly held the lead after making a jackrabbit start. Again accompanied by Bianculli he placed third in their heat and seventh of the 24 entries in the final after sundry vicissitudes.

For the first time, after Necochea, Juan Fangio reckoned his chances as a driver. His performance there, he reflected, 'made me realise that, if I really wanted to, I could take up the career of which I had dreamed intensely for so many years. If I had come in third against well-known, experienced drivers, I could surely improve with a better engine and a bit of luck.' Others noticed too. Reported *El Liberal* about the 'humble lad' from Balcarce: 'A new star has risen in the regional automotive firmament. His name was loudly cheered, as if everyone had recognised a winner who will exceed their expectations.'

Fangio was not yet 27. In the prime of life, blessed with a practical knowledge of the internal workings of automobiles, he could race with the backing of his friends and the wary tolerance of his parents. 'For me the support of family, and especially of my friends in Balcarce, has always been the most important thing,' he said later. 'They helped me immensely from the very beginning, and without them I would never have had the chance to begin my racing.'

Recalled his brother Toto for Carozzo, 'Juan loved our mother and father very much, in fact he adored them. My father more so, perhaps, as I was always closer to mother. Know what it was? Juan spent less time with him, and so scarcely ever contradicted him. After all, we all answer our parents back at some time. Don Loreto had this written on his heart: "My son never answered me back." Juan was very good to my father and he, in his heart of hearts, was pleased that he was a racing driver. But mother suffered a lot.'

In October 1938 Fangio had his first exposure to the gruelling Argentine style of long-distance racing, the Gran Premio Argentino de Carreteras. Two were run that year. Although technically he was a riding mechanic in the second, which covered 4,600 miles in ten stages alternating between transit and timed sections, in fact he did most of the driving. He and Luis Finochietti in a Ford coupé placed a respectable seventh. Although he ran a few more races in his own Ford V8, Fangio would now focus on the increasingly popular Gran Premio events.

Another driver, Oscar Gálvez, made his Gran Premio debut in 1938. Two years younger than Juan Fangio, Gálvez and his younger brother Juan hailed from prosperous Buenos Aires. Their natural choice for the events had been the fast Ford V8 coupé. A Ford was what Juan Fangio had in mind as well when the citizens of Balcarce organised a campaign to raise the money for him to buy a car to race in 1939; some 240 of them contributed. But nary a suitable Ford could be had when Fangio and his friends went shopping.

They found themselves in a Chevrolet agency looking at a shiny black 1939 coupé. Chevrolets were not unknown in the Gran Premio races; General Motors backed their entry officially, but they had not yet rivalled the Fords. Fangio looked at it askance: *'Andará esto?'* he asked. 'Will that thing go?' Go it would have to, so they bought the Chevy and took it to their shop to begin race preparation.

The straight-six Chevrolet engine had the benefit of overhead valves but the deficit of rod-bearing lubrication by scoops in the bottom of the connecting rods that picked up oil from the sump on each crank rotation. Once the wily Fangio turned this feature to his advantage: 'Finding myself short of oil in a minor race, I nonchalantly added water so that the remaining oil would float on it, keeping the level high enough to feed the pickup spoons on the big-ends and circulating with enough pressure to let me finish the race.'

The Chevy threw one oiling problem after another at Fangio. He and his friends licked them, however, both before and during the start of the 1939 Gran Premio and its continuation after atrocious weather forced the abandonment of its first stages. In spite of an off-road excursion when he was in the lead, Fangio finished fifth overall, by far the best-placed Chevrolet. The GM men who had slighted and even hindered him at the start were falling over themselves to offer tyres, help and money by the finish.

Oscar Gálvez was the 1939 winner, with his brother Juan riding shotgun. Two new stars shone that year in the Argentine racing firmament and two stimulating rivalries were born: the *Gálvistas* against the *Fangistas* and the *Fordistas* against the *Chevroletistas*. For a decade their battles would be the stuff of epic legend in Argentina.

The promise Juan Fangio had shown in the Gran Premio of 1939 was realised in 1940 in the most ambitious race of its kind Argentina had ever attempted. To dramatise the coming Pan American Highway the racers would roar north-west from Buenos Aires through the Andes and Bolivia to Lima, Peru, then back again, a round trip of 5,868 miles or almost 10,000 kilometres. From 27 September to 12 October in a race to exhaustion of man and machine Juan Fangio was the winner in his dark-green Chevrolet coupé. With almost 50,000 pesos in prize money he could easily afford, at last, to buy the car he had raced.

Juan Fangio would later name this as his most satisfying race – his first big victory against strong opposition and against fatigue: 'We kept ourselves going by eating cloves of garlic and chewing coca leaves.' Yet at altitude fatigue sometimes threatened to win the battle: 'On the Altiplano I was very tired during the 1940 Gran Premio and on the mountain road I felt attracted by the precipice. At one point I had a terrible temptation to run the wheel toward the edge and to finish with everything.'

All Argentina followed Juan's exploits over Radio Belgrano. 'There was a radio commentator named Luis Sojit,' recalled Gianni Rogliatti. 'This man was fantastic because he used to do the radio transmission for the long races. For 12 hours he would talk continuously with small breaks for advertising.' Small wonder that when Juan was on the last stages into Buenos Aires he was surprised to hear the crowds chanting 'Fan-jo, Fan-jo!' He would hear that chant many times in years to come.

Fangio was Argentina's *Carreteras* ('roads') champion in 1940 and again in 1941 when he won two big events. He was a winner again in 1942 before Eastertime brought an end to Argentine motorsports. Backed by his home-town potato-growers, Fangio turned to the buying of vehicles to get their valuable tyres and to trading in trucks. He was driving long distances to his customers: 'I drove as fast as possible, studying every curve and bend, helped by lack of traffic because of the war. Five years of idleness can make a driver rusty. I fumed with rage as the years rolled by, afraid of being too old when, eventually, races started again. I knew I was driving towards my future, whatever it might hold. I was racing alone, full of nostalgia, blasting up great clouds of dust on deserted roads.'

Frustratingly for Fangio, peacetime came slowly to far-away Argentina. He was indeed idle as a racing driver for five years. On 26 February 1946 a new era began for his country with the election to the presidency of General Juan Domingo Perón, who took office in June. Less than a year later the Argentine Automobile Club realised its dream of attracting some European drivers and racing cars to Buenos Aires in the height of its southern-hemisphere summer to race against the best local talent and machinery. Races would also be held in February 1947 for locally built specials, the class known as *Mecánica Nacional*.

Juan Fangio was caught on the hop. Busy with his wheeling and dealing, he hadn't prepared a suitable car. Brother Toto and partner José Duffard set to work to squeeze a 3.9-litre Chevrolet six into a Model T-based racer they happened to have in the shop. Nicknamed 'Negrita', this ugly beast was Fangio's mount for the first half of the 1947 season. At Buenos Aires he was too exhausted after preparing it to pay much attention to the European flair of Achille Varzi and Luigi Villoresi in their Maseratis. And although he scored one win in 'Negrita' at Rosario, she was not the racing car of his dreams.

'I was in Buenos Aires when I saw a really good-looking *Nacional* for sale,' Fangio remembered, 'called the Volpi. It had an American Rickenbacker engine. By this time I had a good relationship with the Suixtil textile company, which made and marketed a range of sports shirts and gentleman's fashion, and they helped me to buy that car. It handled well but at Bell Ville I found the Rickenbacker engine lacked power, so we replaced it with a Chevrolet, and then the Volpi became a very good car indeed.' The handsome Volpi-Chevrolet was in fact good enough to take him to six victories through the 1949 season.

The lure of the long-distance *Carreteras* was still strong too. Although Fangio won a few of the shorter events after the war he was destined never again to triumph in the long ones in his trusty Chevrolets. Indeed it was worse than that. In a 1948 race from Buenos Aires to Venezuela's Caracas, Juan was bidding to pass Oscar Gálvez when the two cars touched and Fangio's spun off the road. His riding mechanic Daniel Urrutía was fatally injured in the crash. 'That, I think, was my bitterest hour,' Fangio told friends later.

When the next winter season was organised for pure racing cars (no *Nacionals*) in January–February 1948 two 1½-litre supercharged Maseratis were brought from Europe to be driven by local racers. Who would be at their wheels? The Automobile Club interviewed the candidates. Driver after driver asked how much he would earn by racing these cars. One, Juan Manuel Fangio, asked, 'How much will it cost me?' This attitude, plus his skill, earned him a seat.

In the first two 1948 races he fared only moderately well in his Maserati against august visitors like Achille Varzi, 'Nino' Farina, 'Gigi' Villoresi and Jean-Pierre Wimille. For the third and fourth races, however, Fangio was loaned a light and lively Simca-Gordini by

Amédée Gordini. Wimille was driving one too on the tight Rosario circuit, where the two men had a ding-dong battle for the lead after the Gálvez Alfa retired.

'It was a duel between the two of us,' said Fangio. 'I believe the Frenchman was somewhat piqued at the way I was following him. He signalled to me to pass him and I was in front of him for a while, going faster and faster. He passed me again and then I passed him again. By then I knew where on the circuit I could overtake him and win, but the Simca's little engine wouldn't deliver the goods.' Afterward Wimille, then the leader of the Alfa Romeo team in Europe, paid *el Chueco* a tribute: 'Fangio should be put at the wheel of a first-class car and then he would surely do great things.'

For the 1949 *Temporada*, as the winter season was known, the Argentine Auto Club imported two first-class cars, the latest 4CLT/48 Maseratis, low-chassis racers with two-stage supercharging. Also guesting from Europe were Wimille, Farina, Villoresi, Prince Bira, Briton Reg Parnell and a promising newcomer, Alberto Ascari.

A cloud was cast over the meetings by the death in practice of Wimille after a crash in his Gordini. A *Mecánica Nacional* race was dedicated to him; Fangio won it.

The four *Temporada* races saw wins for Ascari, Gálvez, Farina and, in the last race at Mar del Plata, after a hectic battle with Ascari's similar but bigger-engined Maserati, Juan Fangio. Among the crowd of 300,000 at the seaside resort were some 30,000 good folk from Balcarce, only 35 miles away. That Sunday, laughed Fangio, 'The only person in church was the priest.'

Back in Britain, Reg Parnell briefed Rodney Walkerley of *The Motor* on his Argentine adventures. Parnell was 'much impressed by the race fever over there … and by the determined and skilful driving of some of the local talent, particularly this Fangio who won at Mar del Plata … says they all have but one idea: to win the race – and drive accordingly from start to finish.'

For the 1950 *Temporada* the main protagonists were all driving supercharged 2-litre Ferraris. The Argentines were shut out of victories this time, but Fangio was optimistic about his chances for the 1951 races. Knowing that Mercedes-Benz were coming with their great 1939 Grand Prix cars, he and the race organisers conspired to create an ultra-twisty road circuit that would frustrate their power and speed. At the last minute, however, he was asked to drive one of the Mercedes!

Fangio and Mercedes-Benz were beaten in the two 1951 events by José Froilán González in the Ferrari that Fangio had expected to race. The twisty track he had helped to select had played its part, said Juan: 'Sometimes, when you do something you ought not to have done, you get punished for it. God needs no whip to punish, as the saying goes. That's what happened to me.' Fangio would have a later Ferrari for the 1952 *Temporada* races, which he would dominate.

Just before his races for Mercedes-Benz, on Christmas Eve of 1950 Juan Fangio tackled one of Argentina's classic events, the 500 miles of Rafaela. Its golden book listed the great names of Argentine motorsports, Riganti and Zatuszek. Fangio would be at the wheel of one of the three 4½-litre Lago-Talbot Grand Prix cars brought to Argentina by Tony Lago expressly for this race in support of Eva Perón's social fund. Each was fitted with netting in front of the grille to ward off grasshoppers and extra shields next to the windscreen to protect the drivers from the dirt and stones thrown up from the unmade roads.

'At the start,' said French Talbot team leader Louis Rosier, respected as one of Europe's hard men of racing, 'we had to run a team race in order to ensure a Talbot victory. Only then were we able to attack and separate. The race was very hard and very fast. For me, the scorching heat made the race much more exhausting than the 24 Hours of Le Mans.' González retired in one of the blue cars and Rosier's finished a minute and a half behind winner Juan Fangio. Fangio's overpowering endurance was already a legend in South America. Soon it would also be acknowledged, and celebrated, in Europe.

Fangio races his newly acquired Volpi Special at Bell Ville in Córdoba province in July 1947. By August he replaces its 20-year-old American Rickenbacker engine with a trusty Chevrolet and goes on to score six victories through 1949.

At the age of four Juan Fangio poses (opposite) with his sisters Celia and Herminia and his older brother José. Fangio is third from the left in the front row (top) of the Rivadavia football club that encourages him to set up a workshop of his own in Balcarce. Humble though it is, that first workshop (bottom) suffices to put Juan Fangio in business. Labouring under the sign of the star (right), Don Loreto Fangio stays active as a plasterer and stonemason as long as his health allows.

The speed-crazed 'wild bunch' of Balcarce is undeterred by its lack of racing cars. Juan Fangio adopts his most menacing expression as he leans on the shoulder of Bianculli in the racing car they made from a Ford Model A taxi belonging to the latter's father. The year is 1936.

18

Victorious Juan Fangio finishes so far ahead of his rival Oscar Gálvez in the 1941 road race in Brazil that he has time to flag Gálvez home (left). In 1939 Juan is accompanied by Hector Tieri in the Argentine Turismo de Carretera *races that show he is a driver to be reckoned with (above). Fangio returns to* Carretera *racing after the war (right), still faithful to the six-cylinder Chevrolet.*

ALCARCE
HUELLA
LA 2 DULCE

More enthusiast than mechanic – which is why Fangio is doing his own wheel-changing – his friend Daniel Urrutía accompanies Juan in post-war races. They are winning (above and right) the February 1948 race at Vuelta de Pringles in their red Chevrolet Coupé. Fangio called Urrutía's death in a crash later that year 'my bitterest hour'.

Fangio is asked to join Hermann Lang and Karl Kling in the Mercedes-Benz team for two races in Buenos Aires in February 1951. Improperly adjusted for the conditions, the cars don't perform well and Fangio is third in the first race and retires in the second (preceding pages). He is nevertheless well on his way as a Mercedes-Benz dealer, later adding a sales point in Buenos Aires (above). Argentine strongman Juan Perón sympathises with Fangio's problems (right) in the 1951 races to the surprise of the Ferrari-mounted winner of both events, Froilán Gonzáles at left.

Starting from the centre of the grid in its first race, Juan Fangio's brand-new Maserati 4CLT/48 takes him to fourth place at Palermo Park in Buenos Aires on 29 January 1949 (left). When he beats all the Europeans at Mar del Plata on 27 February hysteria is rampant (below). His fans are not slow to show their appreciation of his fine driving (above).

2

CHAPTER 2

'That Fangio'

'When I had finished my lap of honour and shut the engine off while coasting into the pits, I felt entirely transfigured, different somehow. Now I knew that I could do nothing else but race in Grands Prix.' Mar del Plata 1949 had been an epiphany for the 37-year-old Juan Manuel Fangio, he told biographers Federico Kirbus and Ronald Hansen. 'That night I was interviewed by radio and said I hoped that the Automobile Club would send a small team to Europe. I didn't expect to have much chance in Europe, but was hoping that we could win one race at least, which would be wonderful for us.

'A few days later I was called to the Automobile Club in Buenos Aires. When they came to ask me I was in Patagonia, selling trucks. They said they were going to send a team of two Maseratis and two Simca-Gordinis to Europe, and they wanted to know if I was willing to lead the team. Naturally, you can imagine what my answer was.' But deeply committed as he was by now to his businesses, Juan Manuel saw this as a season that would bring him great pleasure and satisfaction – after which he would settle down again at home. One year abroad would be enough.

Juan Fangio retires in his final race in a 4CLT/48 Maserati at Zandvoort in Holland on 23 July 1950. These Argentine Automobile Club Maseratis nevertheless provide the key with which Juan unlocks his European racing career.

Some in the government had been against sending Fangio. They saw him as quiet, self-effacing and diffident, not the kind of ebullient go-getter who would give a high profile to Perón's New Argentina abroad. But Fangio's skill on the track had spoken loudly on his behalf, as had his maturity and practicality. He had demonstrated these qualities during a 1948 reconnaissance mission to the United States and Europe to assess the state of motorsports and the chances Argentina would have abroad.

Underpinning this effort was the determination of the new Perónist Party of Juan Domingo Perón to make Argentina self-sufficient as an automobile producer, no longer relying on the American plutocrats for their assembled Fords and Chevrolets. His popularity bolstered by the public's affection for the legendary 'Evita', his blonde actress wife María Eva Duarte de Perón, Juan Perón used the Automobile Club as one channel for his contacts with European industrialists. Protagonists there were the Club's chief, Carlos Anesi, and his head of motorsports, Francisco Alberto 'Pancho' Borgonovo. 'He opened the gates of Europe for me,' Fangio said of Borgonovo.

On his 1948 trip Fangio was accompanied by an Auto Club official and other drivers including arch-rival Oscar Gálvez. With his dark brilliantined hair, sharp moustache and toothy grin, Gálvez was much more the prototype of the Argentine racing driver, *qua* tango dancer, than the unobtrusive Fangio. A man who had seen both race, experienced team manager Nello Ugolini, rated Gálvez the faster driver. But Gálvez had acquired some heavy baggage during his career, including a reputation as a car breaker and a poor loser who lacked sportsmanship. His would not be the career that Argentina would promote abroad.

The delegation travelled via Los Angeles and Detroit to arrive at Indianapolis in time for the 1948 500-mile race, which made a profound impression on the Argentines. Fangio vowed to return as a competitor one day. They continued to France where they watched fellow countryman Clemar Bucci compete at Monte Carlo and at San Remo, where the new 4CLT/48 Maserati made its successful debut, and then to Paris, where Fangio suffered the embarrassment of losing all his money and papers. Jean-Pierre Wimille came to his aid.

On Paris's Boulevard Victor Juan Fangio knocked on the door of the man who had trusted him with a car in Argentina at the beginning of the year, Amédée Gordini. Fangio's luck – an attribute he would greatly value – was in. Maurice Trintignant, who would have driven one of the Gordinis in the French Grand Prix at Reims, was hospitalised after a crash in Switzerland. A Gordini seat was open.

A less suitable venue could scarcely be imagined. The underpowered Gordinis were no match for the fast Reims road course. 'One of the lads said I wouldn't be able to do much in a little car like that,' Fangio told Carozzo, 'but I replied: "If there's a race in it for me, I'll get into any car." All that race really meant to me was that Amédée Gordini asked me to drive one of his cars. In a way, I was repaying him for his noble deed at Rosario, where he provided me with a car in which I was able to lead a race against European drivers.'

But what had induced the saturnine, chain-smoking Frenchman to entrust a car to the all-but-unknown Fangio? The latter was never sure: 'When he chose me, from among many other Argentine drivers, to take the wheel of one of his single-seaters, I don't know exactly what his guiding motivations were. However, what I do know perfectly is that he awakened me to one of the most intense pleasures of my whole life. Whatever your career, whatever the other joys or other pains, if you love competition you can never forget your first race competing in a Grand Prix car.'

Gordini's was not a prepossessing stable, Fangio recalled: 'His business lived from day to day. Nothing was ready on time. He placed great faith in his own personal mechanical conceptions and he suffered from bad moods from time to time. But this devil of a man knew how to extract the maximum horsepower possible from a piece of machinery. He also knew how to motivate his colleagues to express the best of themselves. Every member of the team had the spirit of a winner.' Every other team he raced for had far greater material resources, Fangio said later, but 'I never again experienced the emotions I felt when in the company of the Equipe Gordini.'

Fangio placed his Simca-Gordini in the middle of the front row for his first European start in the Formula 2 race that preceded the Grand Prix on 18 July 1948. From the Reims flagfall at noon the bigger Ferraris took command, but Fangio held fourth before retiring with a holed fuel tank. This was replaced so that he could start in the Grand Prix proper. Slipstreaming cars with more than triple his Gordini's power, Juan Manuel managed to trail the Alfa Romeos and Lago-Talbots, but the revs thus generated were more than his engine could take. He retired just short of two-thirds distance.

The visitor did not go unnoticed. Rodney Walkerley said that 'his performance with the Simca indicates that he has the real Grand Prix panache.' Fangio also made an observation of his own. A driver whose legendary career he deeply respected, Tazio Nuvolari, took over Villoresi's Maserati for a spell in the French Grand Prix. Nuvolari, then 55, had no influence on the outcome of the race. 'By the time I met him they were exploiting him,' Fangio said of the great Mantuan, 'and the young guys were beating him. I was really displeased about this. I thought that when I retired I would do so before arriving at the point Nuvolari had reached.'

Another great driver of the pre-war era, Achille Varzi, was lost to the sport that summer. In practice for the Swiss Grand Prix he slid off a damp curve in his Alfa Romeo, overturned on an earth bank and was mortally injured. Fangio and his colleagues attended the services for Varzi at his home in Galliate, Italy. This was a poignant loss for the Argentine. Only a few weeks earlier at San Remo Varzi had invited Fangio to join him at the dinner table: 'It was a big honour for me because Varzi had a special charm. He was a champion, but at the same time not easy to approach. Toward me he acted in an affecting way, showing both respect and sympathy. Our friendship was genuine.'

Before returning to Argentina the visitors had negotiated with Maserati to buy the two new 4CLT/48 Grand Prix cars that the Auto Club would offer to drivers, including Fangio, for the 1949 *Temporada* and in which Juan Manuel would score his heartening Mar del Plata victory. In that 1949 winter season, of course, Fangio would find himself again at a wake for a great driver, this time Wimille. Deprived of both Varzi and Wimille and missing also the unwell Count Felice Trossi, Alfa Romeo decided to withdraw its all-conquering Type 158 Grand Prix cars for the 1949 season.

Alfa's withdrawal was good news for the Argentine team setting sail for the Old World to compete in Grand Prix races with their two Maseratis painted in the blue and yellow colours of their country. Picked to partner Fangio was lantern-jawed Benedicto Campos, who had shown mercurial speed in an older Maserati in the winter races. Their first entry would be on 3 April at San Remo, not far from the port at Genoa at which their cars and their small cadre of mechanics arrived.

Thanks to the Varzi connection the young team had good advice and assistance in its race choices and strategy. One of the telegrams Juan Fangio opened before leaving for Europe included this message: 'I OFFER YOU THE SUCCESSION OF MY SON, HIS WORKSHOP, GARAGE AND SMALL HOUSE.' It was from Achille Varzi's father, Menotti Varzi. 'He insisted on our going there,' Fangio said of the facilities at Galliate. 'The Auto Club was naturally overjoyed at the offer. The hospitality we were given there was tremendous, really.' This solution had been engineered by Amedeo Bignami, the shrewd manager-mechanic who had attended Varzi. He managed the race entries for the Argentines, who named their team *Equipo Achille Varzi* in honour of the courtesies they received.

The round-the-houses race at San Remo was familiar territory for Fangio: 'In practice I had quite a struggle with Bira, and Bira made fastest lap in practising on the Friday, although I beat that on the Saturday and set up the best time.' There was only one problem: his Maserati engine lost oil pressure. Fangio himself inspected the failed connecting-rod bearing, polished away the scoring of the rod journal and meticulously fitted a new bearing before going to bed at one in the morning.

In both of the two San Remo heats Fangio rocketed off and led all the way through. 'Bira made the fastest lap,' said Fangio of the very experienced Siamese prince who was driving a similar car and whom he defeated by a minute on aggregate time. In the *Temporada* races Bira had driven to conserve his Maserati far from home. 'Bira in Europe was not the Bira we had seen in Argentina. In Europe he had a big reputation and he hadn't achieved it by going slowly, you may be sure.'

Before boarding the airliner bound for Europe Fangio had said to the press, simply, 'At least one win.' Now, he reflected to Kirbus and Hansen, 'I'd done it already, and a lot sooner than I'd expected. Really I was overjoyed. Of course I'd won in Mar del Plata, but it was entirely different to pull it off in Europe itself, and I felt as if I'd reached the top of the world that time.' Radio Belgrano went into overdrive with the news, broadcast eulogistically to fans at home by Luis Elias Sojit and his brother Manuel who had accompanied the *Equipo* to Europe.

The presence of radio broadcasters was only one of the attributes of the Argentine team that startled Europeans. Rodney Walkerley: 'Fangio is accompanied everywhere by an imposing collection of club officials, pressmen and sundry experts. When not in the driving seat at races he and his équipe all wear bright blue overalls and bright blue American-style baseball caps which strikes the Englishman as a little bizarre.' Fangio was still enjoying the sponsorship of clothing firm Suixtil, which was not shy about putting its products forward.

Also accompanying the team was an ebullient, curvaceous and forthright Argentine lady whom many took to be Mrs Fangio. Andreina, 'Beba' for short, was Fangio's feminine companion that season and for many more, but they were not married. She and Fangio were befriended that year by one of racing's most engaging characters, Belgian Johnny Claes. A jazzman as well as a racing driver, Claes called his band 'Johnny Claes and his Clay Pigeons'. Six years younger than Fangio, Claes took him under his wing and helped the naturally shy Argentine become better known in Europe.

'His entourage is large and efficient,' Rodney Walkerley wrote of Fangio. 'His mechanics are first class, no expense appears to be spared, the cars are perfectly prepared and the pit is well run.' That was the external impression – a fine advertisement for Perón's Argentina – but under the water the blue and yellow ducks were paddling furiously. 'We all learnt a lot about the cars in those days,' Fangio admitted. 'We didn't know very much about maintenance of Grand Prix cars, and had to learn the hard way. That meant that our Maseratis were soon in need of a good overhaul.

'After San Remo we had a victory dinner,' Juan Manuel added, 'and one of the champagne corks flying through the air landed in my lap. This is considered a very good omen in Argentina, and Benedicto told me to keep it as it would bring me luck. It did so until Marseilles, but in the rush of leaving that city I lost it – and lost the next race! What a curious coincidence!'

His next victory after San Remo was two weeks later at Pau in France. Fangio: 'I won against more or less the same crowd. Emanuel de Graffenried gave me a pretty good race. Campos was third there, as well, and driving much more wisely than I thought he would.'

In fact Fangio had to make a mid-race pit stop at Pau to top up the oil tank of his Maserati, a model which had a well-deserved reputation for leaking oil. Officials ordered the engine to be stopped during this manoeuvre and the mechanic assigned to start it again made no headway with the hand crank. Fangio jumped out of the cockpit, pushed the man aside and with one sharp pull had it going again. 'One way and another it was an unusual day,' he recalled. 'The band didn't have the music of the Argentine anthem so they played some Brazilian march.'

It was a battle with Bira again in May at Perpignan over two heats. There Fangio won the first heat by enough of a margin that he could afford to finish half a car-length behind the Siamese in the second heat to win overall. By now Argentina, whipped to white heat by the Sojit brothers, was agog over the adventures of their racing emissaries. 'The enthusiasm was so great,' wrote Robert Carozzo, 'that the musician Javier Mazzea composed his tango "Fangio" for the radio. The singer Alberto Castillo had only two hours in which to learn it and practise it a bit with his orchestra before going on the air with it. This was on the day of the man from Balcarce's fourth victory.'

The fourth win in a row came at Marseilles in a race for unsupercharged racing cars. The tortuous town circuit was perfect for the two Gordinis that the *Equipo Achille Varzi* had added to its strength. Juan Fangio was second in his heat behind a car with an engine three times bigger, Philippe Etancelin's Lago-Talbot, which he defeated in the final race in a virtuoso display of driving. He paid tribute to his mount: 'The Simca was a very neat car, very short wheelbase, very well adapted to tight circuits, and very light. Gordini was perhaps the first European constructor to give much importance to power-to-weight ratio. That's how he was able to win races with cars of scarcely 1,430cc.'

Marseilles had given Fangio another glimpse of the twilight of the great career of Tazio Nuvolari. Already weakened by the illness that would kill him, Nuvolari managed only a single lap. Fangio's resolve to quit while at the top was further reinforced.

The *Equipo*'s next Formula 1 race was on the challenging Belgian Spa circuit in June. The team's Maseratis were tired. 'By this time things were a bit rough,' Juan told Kirbus and Hansen. 'We'd practically run out of money, and furthermore the Maseratis were by this time simply crying for factory attention. Benedicto and I did a few laps in the Belgian Grand

Prix to collect starting money, but we knew very well neither of us stood a chance during the race, although we wound up the machines during practising and got away with some decent practice laps.' Juan started in the front row but retired with a broken valve on the second lap.

In the meantime they'd been impressed by the speed of the 2-litre V12 Ferraris in the races at Marseilles and at Rome's Caracalla circuit, where Juan drove a ropy Maserati and retired. The call went out to Pancho Borgonovo to see whether the Auto Club was up to buying a Ferrari or two for the Argentine team. Miraculously it was. Fangio took the wheel of a Ferrari for the first time in a test at Modena's Autodromo.

At Monza for the Formula 2 Grand Prix Fangio found himself facing the newer factory Ferraris of Ascari and Villoresi. He stripped and fixed his troublesome gearbox himself during practice. In his first drive on the great Monza road course the works Ferraris did Fangio the honour of retiring, but he found himself racing Felice Bonetto in a private Ferrari and his oil-temperature needle moving inexorably upward. Treading the high wire between the two he won the race and collected the fastest lap as well. The prize money paid for the overhauls that the Maseratis desperately needed.

Refreshed, the Maseratis were ready for the Grand Prix on the fast Albi road course in July. In the qualifying heat Fangio faced, for the first time in Europe, a man he greatly respected: Giuseppe 'Nino' Farina in a similar car. He beat Farina to win his heat, and won the final as well ahead of Prince Bira. On another fast circuit at Reims Fangio and Campos took turns leading the French Grand Prix until Juan Manuel retired with a broken throttle rod; later Campos's engine expired. Fangio easily led the Reims Formula 2 race in the Auto Club's new Ferrari until his gearbox played up.

Thus ended Fangio's European summer of '49. 'This was a marvellous period in my life,' he reflected. 'I was truly happy. Physically, I was in better form than ever. I recuperated from racing tension by long nights of sleep, going to bed early and sleeping a solid 12 hours to be ready to face the next day.' His idea of just one season in Europe was now history for Juan Manuel after the great success he'd enjoyed: 'I never thought I'd go to Europe and I never dreamed I'd be successful. It took an effort not to let it all go to my head. I knew I would go on racing. It was my life now, and I would go the whole way, right to the end.'

In *The Motor* Rodney Walkerley sought to sum up the impact of the man: 'Streaking like a meteor across the motor racing firmament this summer was Juan Manuel Fangio and, like the meteor, he has disappeared below the horizon and has gone home to his native Argentina trailing a tail of glory. [He earned] a reputation for driving as fast as possible from start to finish of a race, sliding all his corners and giving very little quarter – in fact, motor racing all the time. His braking is finished long before the curve begins and after that the right foot is hard down through the bend. Fangio is the specialist in cornering on the slide and in the use of wide throttle in all gears at all times.

'Fangio himself is an extremely quiet chap,' continued Walkerley, 'short, thick-set, extremely powerful, dark-haired, beefy and speaks with a surprisingly high, small voice rather reminiscent of Rudy Caracciola. He is about 35 years of age, unmarried, friendly, modest and drives like a demon.' As a capsule summary of the Juan Fangio of 1949 this could hardly be surpassed.

A close student of motor racing found something wanting in the early Fangio technique. 'At first,' wrote Denis Jenkinson, 'Fangio's driving style was not very good to watch. Though it had all the speed and panache of Raymond Sommer, it did not have the elegance of Ascari or Farina, or the delicacy and finesse of Maurice Trintignant or Prince Bira.' Fangio admitted that it took him some time to master the Maseratis: 'The cars I'd raced on the road were so heavy and unresponsive, slow compared with the ones I found in Europe. The Grand Prix cars required much more delicacy to drive.'

'At the end of that season,' 'Jenks' acknowledged, 'I wrote in one of my motor racing books, "To those of us who have been fortunate enough to see this Fangio in action, the fact that he scored a hat-trick with his first three appearances in European racing does not come as such a surprise, for he really 'motor races' with his Maserati in a manner that is a joy to behold."'

That 1949 season marked the beginning of an appreciation in Europe of Fangio's qualities as described in

Autosport by Gregor Grant: 'Soon the racing folk began to realise that this quiet, blue-eyed man was not only a very great driver, but also that his general attitude to the game was entirely different to that often possessed by highly publicised stars. He had not an ounce of personal conceit, was intensely loyal to his employers and, above all, was completely free from the petty jealousies that invariably go with a continual striving for recognition.' They knew this at home, of course; now they were coming to understand it abroad as well.

On 25 August Juan Fangio flew back to an Argentina that greeted him exultantly as its new sporting hero. A huge crowd hailed him at the airport and another cheered him at the presidential palace, the *Casa Rosada*, where he was received by Juan Perón. Late that night he was the guest of honour at a reception and dinner hosted by Suixtil, which had met many of the costs of the trip. Few encomiums touched Fangio more than a banner he saw at the airport: 'Gálvez fans salute the champion Fangio.' Its bearers reached across the gap of their intense rivalry to salute his achievements in Europe.

Fangio told his fans that he had been made an offer for the 1950 season by Alfa Romeo, which was considering a return to the tracks. At the time he said he was unsure about accepting because he wanted more freedom of action than Alfa was willing to provide. Ultimately he gained the scope he wanted because he continued to compete in Europe in 1950 in the Argentine Auto Club's cars in events not entered by Alfa Romeo.

Back in Europe in March 1950 Juan placed a close third in the Marseilles race in the Club Ferrari, then in April won a Formula 1 race from pole at Pau in the Maserati. This was his last win in the supercharged 4CLT/48 that had done so much to make his name.

Accompanying Fangio in the Club's cars this season was Froilán González, who retired at Pau. (Campos had blotted his copybook with some self-serving acts on and off the circuits late in the 1949 season.) Another victory was logged at Angoulême in June with a 4CLT/48 that the Argentines had opportunistically fitted with a 2-litre unsupercharged Maserati six. Fangio was second in a heat at Albi with a 4CLT/48 but couldn't start in the final.

May of 1951 found Fangio again in some of the cars that had started his single-seater career. He retired at Monza in an Auto Club Ferrari and drove again for Amédée Gordini in Paris's Bois de Boulogne, where he led and set fastest lap but was put out by a dropped valve.

Car builders who had given Fangio their early support were also rewarded by his willingness to drive for them in a race that some Formula 1 drivers avoided, the 24 Hours of Le Mans. There in 1950 Gordini had the services of both Fangio and González to drive a charming little coupé with a supercharged 1½-litre engine. They pedalled it to an astonishing ninth place but retired in the early laps with ignition failure. In 1951 Juan was partnered with Louis Rosier in a Lago-Talbot like the one both men had raced at Rafaela at the end of 1950 – plus wings and lights. Among the early leaders, they had to retire when their oil tank split.

By the end of 1951 'that Fangio' was world champion driving for Alfa Romeo. But 1949 was the year that made his name in Europe – and, through the press, in the world outside Argentina. Fangio had indeed stepped into the shoes of those great lost drivers who had generously recognised his merits: Jean-Pierre Wimille and Achille Varzi.

Paced by the ebullient Frenchman Raymond Sommer (24) in a works Ferrari, Juan Fangio leads the field in his Maserati (18) at the start of the first heat at San Remo on 3 April 1949. Against a strong entry he is the surprise overall winner.

Fangio leads again from the start of the second heat at San Remo in April 1949 (opposite top). Chasing him is Siamese prince B. Bira (34) who places second overall, next to Bonetto's Ferrari (42). Bira gives Fangio a tussle (opposite bottom) at Perpignan in May, but Juan, second here, takes the victory.

His Argentine-entered Maserati still pristine, Juan Fangio pilots it to victory at Pau in France on 18 April 1949, his second victory in a row in Europe (above). He is flagged to a victorious finish after 194 miles of racing on the streets of Pau by Charles Faroux. Although Fangio qualifies to start from the middle of the front row in the Belgian Grand Prix in June (overleaf) his tired Maserati soon expires and Talbot-mounted Louis Rosier wins.

PNEU
STANDARD
CHAMPION

NGLEBERT
VANGUARD
Esso
ESSENCES
HUILES
Firestone
FERODO

Fangio and his colleagues: Juan concentrates as Hans Stuck explains the AFM he will race at Monza in 1950 (above). At Le Mans in 1951 (top left) Louis Rosier (left) joins the Argentines, who are wearing a job lot of jackets. Young Onofre Marimon is on the right next to Froilán Gonzáles. Fangio compares notes with Ferrari rival Gonzáles at the 'Ring in 1951 (centre left) and listens with poorly disguised scepticism to his team-mate Benedicto Campos at Marseilles in 1949 (left).

Among the key protagonists in Juan Fangio's early seasons in single-seaters are (above) Karl Kling on the left with Hermann Lang, Amédée Gordini (above right), with whom Fangio is having a conversation years later, Prince Bira of Siam (right), runner-up at Perpignan, and Alberto Ascari (below), whom Fangio is congratulating on his victory in the 1950 Grand Prix of Modena.

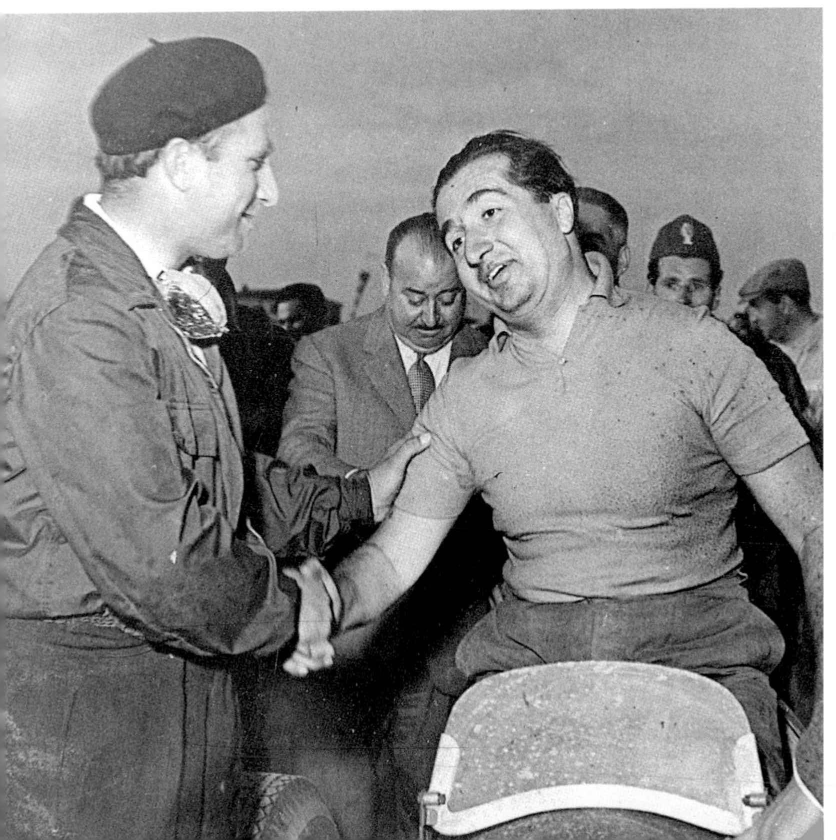

When Fangio finds that the new V12 Ferraris are the quick Formula 2 cars, the Argentine Automobile Club acquires one for its European team. Fangio's first Ferrari drive at Monza in June of 1949 (left) is rewarded with a well-judged victory. His luck with this car is less good at the Modena Autodromo in May 1950 (overleaf), when he retires. In a Monza Formula 2 race in May 1950 (above) Fangio is third in his heat in the blue Ferrari with its yellow bonnet, but retires in the final.

Amédée Gordini reaches out to Fangio, not only to offer him rides in Argentina but also to provide his first European single-seater drive at Reims on 18 July 1948 (above). Fangio starts and retires twice on that historic day. Racing in the beautiful Parc Borély in Marseilles in May 1949 (below and left) Fangio's little Gordini has the legs of much more powerful racing cars. He gets the cup, the flowers and the lady.

CHAPTER 3

First of the Flying Fs

Alfa Romeo towered over its Grand Prix rivals of the 1940s like Gulliver in the land of the Lilliputians. Owned since the early 1930s by the Italian state, Milan-based Alfa was a renowned – if small – producer of passenger cars of the upper category, cars with a distinct sporting flavour and advanced technology. In the decade before the war Alfa Romeo had been the only company able to offer a serious challenge to the silver Grand Prix cars from Germany. And in the big sports-car races like Le Mans and the Mille Miglia a rakish red Alfa was odds-on to win.

To be able to compete in the *Voiturette* class for 1 1/2-litre cars, increasingly popular across the continent, Alfa Romeo commissioned the design and build of a suitable racer from the stable that entered its cars, the Scuderia Ferrari. Logically called the 158 after its 1 1/2 litres and eight in-line cylinders, the new car was ready in 1938. At Leghorn in July it was victorious in its first race. The elegant new car was soon nicknamed 'Little Alfa' or *'Alfetta'*. But it was a big-time performer.

Fangio takes to the Type 158 Alfa Romeo 'Alfetta' as if it has been made for him. His win in the Belgian Grand Prix at Spa in June 1950 is his second in a championship race for Alfa. Resented outsider though the Argentine may be among his Italian team-mates, he quickly proves his worth.

Nino Farina won the Alfetta's last pre-war race in May 1940 at Tripoli and was at the wheel again in July 1946 when Alfas won their second race after the war at Geneva. The rule-makers had the Alfettas in mind when they matched 1 1/2-litre supercharged cars against 4 1/2-litre unblown racers in the first post-war Formula 1. Responding to the challenge, the Type 158s kept on winning. With such drivers as Wimille, Varzi and Trossi in their cockpits, they raced four times in 1947 and four times in 1948 – winning on every occasion against the Maseratis, Ferraris and Talbots.

Whenever and wherever the Alfettas appeared they were expected to win. As we know they sat out the 1949 season after the deaths in crashes of Varzi and Wimille and, early that year of illness, Count Carlo Felice Trossi. Finances were a factor too; with the aid of Marshall Plan dollars Alfa Romeo was rebuilding its factories and launching its new 1900 saloon. But for 1950 the racing authorities made Alfa an offer it couldn't refuse: the creation of a new world championship for Formula 1 drivers. It simply couldn't stay away.

But where would Alfa find drivers to match its cars? Occasionally the swarthy Consalvo Sanesi would be given the wheel, but his value was greater as the works test driver. Veteran Luigi Fagioli, then 51, was signed, as was the elegant, experienced, fast and determined Nino Farina, 43, good Italians both. Surely Italy would have one more driver able to do justice to these cars? Ascari, Villoresi and Taruffi, all of whom had driven Alfettas in the past, were committed to Ferrari. Triggering intense controversy in Italy, the third front-line Type 158 would be driven by a 38-year-old Argentine, Juan Manuel Fangio.

Juan Manuel thought he knew how the opportunity arose, he told Roberto Carozzo: 'The competition manager of Alfa Romeo had seen me race at San Remo in 1949, when I won my first race in Europe. I don't know quite what happened. I must have made a good impression on him.' He could hardly have failed to notice the spectacular swathe sliced through the 1949 season by 'that Fangio'. Alfa Romeo had another motive as well: Argentina, with its influential Italian community, was an important market for Italian products. The choice of Fangio greatly pleased Perón.

Fangio was not a pushover, however. He wanted to be sure that Alfa had no objection to his competing in races in which it was not entering. He couldn't aspire to Number One status ahead of Italy's pride, Farina, but he wanted to be sure he would have a good chance to race for championship points. Returning to Italy in March 1950, Fangio met with Alfa's chief, Dr Antonio Alessio, to discuss these issues. After they reached agreement in principle a dramatic moment followed, as Kirbus and Hansen heard from Fangio:

'Then Dr Alessio took us over the factory to the racing department, where a row of shrouded figures lay in deathly silence, as at a morgue. Alessio lifted the shroud from one of the cars and my excited eyes saw for the first time a Type 158 Alfa Romeo. What a beauty! I got into the seat, and although it had not been adjusted for me it fitted me like a glove. I longed to try it, even to drive it up and down the street outside, but it was not to be. After a few moments I regretfully climbed out and the shroud was replaced.'

Juan Manuel had not yet signed his contract when Alfa entered two cars in a non-championship race at San Remo as a low-key warm-up for the season. It was a circuit he knew; he had won there the year before. But Farina, injured in a previous race, was not available. Ferrari was there in force with Ascari and Villoresi. Alfa was faced with either withdrawing from an event that its promoters had heavily sold on the strength of its first comeback race, or risking its unbeaten reputation on the unproven ability of a foreigner who had not yet even driven a 158!

'They really wanted to pull out of the race,' said Juan, 'but I was obviously keen to take my chance, so I told them, "Look, if I lose, it's Fangio the unknown driver who loses, not Alfa Romeo. But if I win it's Alfa Romeo who wins, providing an unbeatable car for the unknown driver."' They granted him a few practice laps on the wet Saturday and finally agreed to let him have a go on the Sunday.

Although he had won a front-row starting position Fangio was unused to getting off the line with the powerful Alfa. On a still-damp San Remo street he sat with wheelspin as the others rushed away. It looked like the naysayers would win the day. 'Those two or three opening laps were about the worst in my life,' Fangio recalled, 'but gradually I got a grip on myself and almost by itself the little Alfa seemed to go faster and faster, and to my intense relief I gradually managed to get through and win the race. Those were very, very sticky moments.'

The Alfa men fell all over themselves to say that they had always been sure he could do it. 'Dr Alessio wanted me to sign the contract afterwards in the hotel,' said Fangio, 'but said, "First we have to agree what money you want." I just signed, and told him to fill in the noughts. I think they were very surprised, but I thought that was right. They were the greatest Grand Prix team in the world and they were giving me the chance to drive their fantastic car. I felt like a singer suddenly invited to perform at La Scala di Milano or the Metropolitan in New York or the Colon in Buenos Aires. It was the happiest moment in my life.'

Fangio's next drive for Alfa was in a two-seater, an experimental 2½-litre coupé in the 1950 Mille Miglia.

Its roof was so low that a major risk was being knocked out over the bumps, especially for his tall riding mechanic Zanardi. 'In the mountains near l'Aquila it began to rain,' Fangio recalled, 'and I slid in a corner. When I regained control after quite a long slide I was so pleased I let out a great whoop and then noticed Zanardi grinning at me. He told me later that my whoop convinced him he was riding with a wild Indian from the pampas!' Zanardi and Fangio would forge a close working relationship after finishing third overall in the Argentine's first attempt at Italy's version of a town-to-town race.

The world championship began in May in Britain, where Juan's Alfetta suffered a rare retirement: 'My only personal satisfaction that day was being presented, with the other twenty drivers, to His Majesty King George VI, who attended the race with the entire Royal Family. I remember that the King wore a dark iron-grey suit with stripes and the Queen had a pleasant smile.' He gained more satisfaction a week later at Monte Carlo for the 11th running of the Grand Prix of Monaco. Racing ahead of a second-lap crash, Fangio scored a resounding victory a lap ahead of Ascari and collected his first world championship points.

In 1950 Alfa Romeo maintained its astonishing record: it won every race it entered, 11 victories in 11 starts. One of its drivers would indeed be world champion, but which one? Among the Three Fs only one failed to win a race, the doughty Fagioli. It wasn't for want of help from Fangio. At Pescara, where he had won in 1933 and 1934, Fagioli was leading when, almost in sight of the finish, his left front suspension collapsed. Fangio in second hung back, not wanting to deny Luigi the well-deserved win that the team had promised him. But behind both of them Rosier's Talbot was gaining. Juan had to pass Fagioli to secure the win for Alfa.

Fagioli had been second on the challenging Spa circuit, where Fangio won. The order was the same in a hot race at Reims that decimated the opposition. A week later two Alfas went to Bari in southern Italy to compete in a non-championship event, the famous race in which Moss in an HWM placed a plucky third behind the two red cars. Leading, the haughty Farina gesticulated sharply at Moss, who had dared to pass his Alfa in a turn. Fangio, who had seen it all, was laughing heartily when he passed the HWM.

Fangio respected but did not admire the fiery Farina style at the wheel. 'I cannot understand how Farina didn't die earlier,' he said. 'When I followed him in the Alfa Romeo it was incredible; he drove like a madman. We used to say that he was protected by the Madonna, but even the Holy Madonna's patience has a limit and he should have considered that she could not be at his disposal all the time.'

The Three Fs led the new world championship before the final race at Monza, the Italian Grand Prix. Fangio led Fagioli by two points and Farina by four, so all he had to do at Monza was trail Farina – only they were driving the latest high-boost Alfettas – and the championship was his. Surprisingly they were challenged in practice by Alberto Ascari in the latest unsupercharged 4½-litre Ferrari, but Fangio just outsped him for pole.

'The start was shattering,' reported Rodney Walkerley. 'The 70,000 spectators were on their feet shouting themselves hoarse. Forty Argentine enthusiasts unfurled a "Viva Fangio" banner in the stand but the uproar was swamped in the vibrating roar of the massed cars as they surged off the grid in a solid phalanx of shining metal and spinning wheels.'

Putting his plan into action, Fangio was comfortably third behind Farina and Ascari's Ferrari, which soon retired. But this time the Argentine was let down by his Alfa. After a burst tyre and a holed radiator he had to retire. He took over Taruffi's Alfetta, which was lying second, but that then broke its engine. He would be second, not first, behind Farina in the inaugural world championship for drivers.

From October to March Juan Fangio was back in Argentina for the winter racing season and a check on his business interests. Over that winter, when he raced a pre-war Mercedes-Benz with Lang and Kling, he and his partners took advantage of his soaring reputation and growing prosperity by opening a Mercedes showroom in Buenos Aires, complete with YPF petrol station. His return to the cockpit of an Alfetta in 1951 was assured; Alfa Romeo intended to defend its title and Fangio was a key weapon in its armoury.

Over the winter the Alfa Romeo engineers and mechanics worked long hours to improve the performance of their Grand Prix cars. They feared not only the Ferrari challenge, which was ominous by the end of 1950, but also Britain's nationally backed racer, the supercharged V16 BRM. This highly publicised 'wonder car' was expected to work miracles when it reached the track. Alfa hoped for fewer pit stops for refuelling with the Alfetta's new larger fuel tanks.

A key contributor to Alfa's challenge was Battista Guidotti, its hugely experienced racing manager. Fangio was also happy to see Gioachino Colombo on the Alfa strength, the man who had designed the original Type 158. 'When Colombo the engineer returned to Alfa Romeo after working for Ferrari it made a big difference,' Fangio said. 'It could be seen in the way the cars were modified and also in the co-ordination of work in the pits.' Changes in the car for 1951 were sufficient to justify the new type number of 159.

For Juan Manuel a vital link with the Alfa team was the chief mechanic on his car, Zanardi. Although Zanardi had accused Fangio of being a 'wild Indian' during their 1950 Mille Miglia drive, in fact it was the stoop-shouldered Italian who looked more like a native American with his bold, dark, big-toothed features. Juan Fangio considered it essential to have an experienced mechanic who was dedicated to him and his car; Zanardi was the choice and theirs was an intimate partnership.

Back in Milan Fangio and Beba settled into the Albergo Columbia on the Via Carlo Tenca, not far from the main railway station, the Piazza della Repubblica and, as fate would have it, the Corso Buenos Aires. Nearby as well was Il Cavalieri, the restaurant where the Achille Varzi team let its hair down at the end of each season. The Columbia was a modest four-storey hostelry they would always use as their European base. They came to know it because an Argentine pioneer in European racing, Clemar Bucci, had first stayed there. There they were well known, appreciated and catered for; that was all they required.

Alfa expected a challenge from BRM at its first 1951 race, a non-championship event on the flat concrete of Silverstone, but the miracle racers were nowhere to be seen. Farina and Fangio comfortably won their heats but in the International Trophy final the heavens opened and the race had to be abandoned after six laps. At the time Britain's Reg Parnell was in the lead in a Ferrari; only the fact that waterlogged Silverstone was declared a 'non-race' preserved the still-unbroken string of Alfa Romeo victories.

The first *mano a mano* between Alfa and Ferrari of 1951 was a championship race in Berne's daunting Bremgarten. Fangio took pole ahead of Farina, but Villoresi, in one of the 4½-litre Ferraris was next to them on the front row. On race day the rains came to Switzerland as well, an added hazard for the high-revving, high-boosted Alfas. But Juan Manuel was up to the job. In spite of having to pit for fuel while Farina ran non-stop, Fangio was the winner of a hard race with Farina third behind Taruffi's Ferrari. Their battle, Juan said with typical dry humour, 'brought the crowds to their feet and stole my limelight.'

In the next month, June, they met again at Spa for the Belgian Grand Prix. For a change the weather was good. Speeds were so fast in practice that Guidotti asked for some 19-inch wheels and suitable Pirellis to be sent from Milan to replace the usual 17-inch rear wheels so the engines wouldn't over-rev at the 180mph-plus they were reaching on the Masta Straight. They arrived just before the cars were gridded.

From pole position Juan made a poor start, with excessive wheelspin, giving Farina and Villoresi the advantage. Two laps after Farina had a refuel and fresh rear Pirellis Fangio did the same – with dramatic consequences. The right rear was easily changed but the splines of the left-hand wheel wouldn't let go. 'Mechanics slaved with hammers, levers and even bare hands,' reported Rodney Walkerley, 'but that wheel would not budge. In the end they undid the brake drum and took the whole thing off. Then they fitted the new tube and cover to the old rim, put the brake drum back, refitted the wheel and sent him back after almost a quarter of an hour.'

During all this mayhem Fangio displayed an insouciance that had onlookers agog. Sipping a mineral water, he poured some over his head to cool off on a warm day in the Ardennes. He belied the image of the fiery Latin with a demeanour that displayed all the anxiety and impatience of a man waiting for the chemist to fill his prescription.

'That day people said how calm I was in the pits as I saw my chances of a win slipping away,' he told Denis Jenkinson. 'It was not me they were slipping away from. I had done everything as it should be done and made no mistake. I believe that someone might well get nervous, or at least uneasy, when he has made a mistake. That was not the case with me. I was calm, even though Farina was at the top of the championship table. The next race of the championship was soon to come.'

The full Ferrari challenge had not yet matured because Alberto Ascari had been off form in the early races after a previous injury. For the next championship Grand Prix on the ultra-fast Reims circuit a new man was seen in the Ferrari pits: none other than Juan Manuel's countryman, sometime team-mate and frequent rival, José Froilán González. Hitherto González had been trundling round the Grand Prix circuits in a Lago-Talbot, a car not at all suited to his impetuous style. He had been drafted in to replace the unwell Piero Taruffi. Granted, one always had the sense that a Ferrari driver was unwell if Enzo said so.

Grand Prix races were long then. At Reims drivers and cars faced 77 laps of a 4.86-mile road course, adding up to 374 miles, on a cloudlessly hot July day. Ascari's Ferrari grabbed an early lead but soon succumbed to his pace. This cleared the way for Fangio, starting from pole, but his Alfetta then stuttered to a stop with magneto trouble. Both drivers now waited for a team-mate to pit so they could take over his car, permissible under the championship rules. Fangio took Fagioli's and Ascari the Ferrari of González, who had impressed everyone with his press-on pace.

'Cornering on the limit and at least once on the grass, in breathtaking slides' (Walkerley), Juan Manuel battled back into the lead with a string of record laps. After three hours and 22 minutes his lead at the finish was just under a minute ahead of the stubborn Ascari. Successful though the Alfa strategy had been, Fagioli was irate at being sidelined. He left the team – in fact left Grand Prix racing altogether – and was replaced by Felice Bonetto, whose job was to keep an Alfetta high and healthy enough for Fangio or Farina to take it over if need be.

Two weeks later at the British Grand Prix González was not asked to give up his V12 Ferrari. Although allocated a 1950 chassis without the latest engine, he revelled in Silverstone's flat, fast turns and put it on pole. Juan Fangio managed to pass him to take the lead but was unable to consolidate an advantage over the hard-charging Froilán: 'We passed and re-passed and I was in the lead when I had to re-fuel. I didn't need a tankful but the pit staff topped it up anyway, which made the car too heavy for me to catch Froilán again.' Juan tried to put pressure on the less-fit González but the Alfa was not up to the job. José Froilán ran out the winner in his Ferrari, administering the first defeat to the Alfas in a full-length race since they lost at St Cloud in June 1946.

Their next encounter was in the 1951 German Grand Prix. 'That was the first time I had seen the Nürburgring,' Fangio said. 'I loved it from the first day. It was a fantastic challenge. I drove round it lap after lap in my 2½-litre Alfa road car to learn it all. I tried to learn it section by section and tried to remember in particular the fast parts, because the slow sections were like driving through the mountains, which I was very accustomed to doing.

'The Ferraris in practice made better time than our Alfas,' Fangio added. 'Trying to beat the lap record just set by Ascari I almost had a serious accident, going off the road on the hill leading down to Adenau. I knew there was an extremely steep drop just beyond the corner where my car began to skid, and came on to it as though leaping from a springboard. By chance, a tree trunk stopped the machine as I managed to swing across the road. No damage to the car and not even a scratch on me. All alone, I put the car back on the road.'

The great form of Ascari and Ferrari in practice was repeated in the race. Fangio led some laps but not the most important ones, the last few, when his Alfetta was not wholly healthy. He was in fact Alfa Romeo's only finisher among four cars; people began to grasp that this was a driver who, although staggeringly fast, also had an exceptional ability to get an ailing car through to a respectable finish.

Although they had met many times before, this race on the 'Ring could be seen as the first of many great battles between Fangio and Ascari. Said the Argentine, 'I had tremendous affection for Ascari, who led the Ferrari team for so many years. I deeply admired the graceful, pleasant style of Alberto's driving. He was a real champion and merited the title for his class, worthy in every way of his father's. I felt it was a great honour to have him as a rival.' The senior Ascari, who had led the Alfa Romeo team in the 1920s, had been a role model for the young Enzo Ferrari.

Fangio won his next clash with Ascari at Bari, a non-championship tune-up for the Italian GP at Monza. There Alberto was the easy winner after three of the four Alfas were out by half distance, including the Type 159 with which pole-sitter Fangio had annihilated the lap record during practice. Still open, the championship would be decided between Fangio and Ascari in the season's last race on the wide avenues of Barcelona.

The sudden ascent at Ferrari of González, who now lay third in the championship, posed problems for Alfa Romeo. At the end of this highly charged season every advantage counted. The rivalry between Milan and Maranello was peaking intensely. Could Alfa be sure that Fangio would not leak the odd racing secret to his compatriot, who was a friend as well as an opponent? It was seen by Alfa as a significant risk.

Fitted with the biggest fuel tanks they had ever carried, the 159s at Barcelona looked ready to run the race non-stop. Noting this, Ferrari decided to equip its cars with smaller 16-inch wheels and tyres that would increase their acceleration. Ascari took pole ahead of Fangio, so this seemed to be working. But just before the start – too late for Fangio to say anything to González – Colombo took his driver aside and told him that they would have to refuel after all. In fact their real plan was to run relatively light and make *two* fuel stops – not unlike Formula 1 strategy of the 1990s.

This worked a treat. Almost immediately the Ferraris were in trouble with their tyres, which were throwing treads. Fangio: 'I saved my tyres all the time, sliding not at all. I don't think they even had to fit new tyres to my car in the pits. If Ferrari had known we were going to stop they would have used the larger tyres and beaten us but we were much faster on the straight for the first time that season and that was how I won in Barcelona – and won my first world championship.' In the final world standings Ascari was just one point ahead of González in second and Farina was fourth.

This was a heady moment for the man from Balcarce: 'I was brought before General Franco's representative, who gave me the cup for the Grand Prix of Spain. I found myself face-to-face with Sojit, the giant-sized Argentine radio reporter who had glued millions of our compatriots to their loudspeakers with his exciting reporting.' The Sojits had the greatest story they had ever broadcast and they made the most of it.

In his first season with Alfa Romeo Juan Fangio had shown he had the speed and judgement needed to lead this great team. In his second season he demonstrated the shrewd racecraft and dominant form that would make him famous. 'There were some wonderful races between Alfa and Ferrari,' he reflected. 'In sentimental terms the Alfetta was perhaps my favourite car of all, because it gave me the chance to be world champion for the first time.' If cars could speak, the Alfetta would have said that the feeling was mutual.

One of the most beautiful racing cars of all time, the Alfetta is also renowned for its championship-class reliability. In the 1950 Swiss Grand Prix, which he leads in the early laps, its electrics let Fangio down, but the other two 'Fs' fill the first and second places.

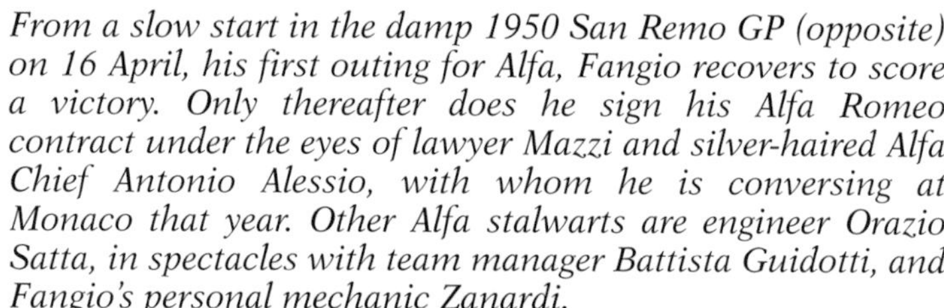

From a slow start in the damp 1950 San Remo GP (opposite) on 16 April, his first outing for Alfa, Fangio recovers to score a victory. Only thereafter does he sign his Alfa Romeo contract under the eyes of lawyer Mazzi and silver-haired Alfa Chief Antonio Alessio, with whom he is conversing at Monaco that year. Other Alfa stalwarts are engineer Orazio Satta, in spectacles with team manager Battista Guidotti, and Fangio's personal mechanic Zanardi.

FERMATA

First you see them, then you don't: the crowds disperse to prepare for the start at Reims in the 1950 French GP. The 'Three Fs' dominate the front row, with winner Fangio nearest the camera, Farina (seventh but not classified) in the middle and Fagioli (second) on the outside.

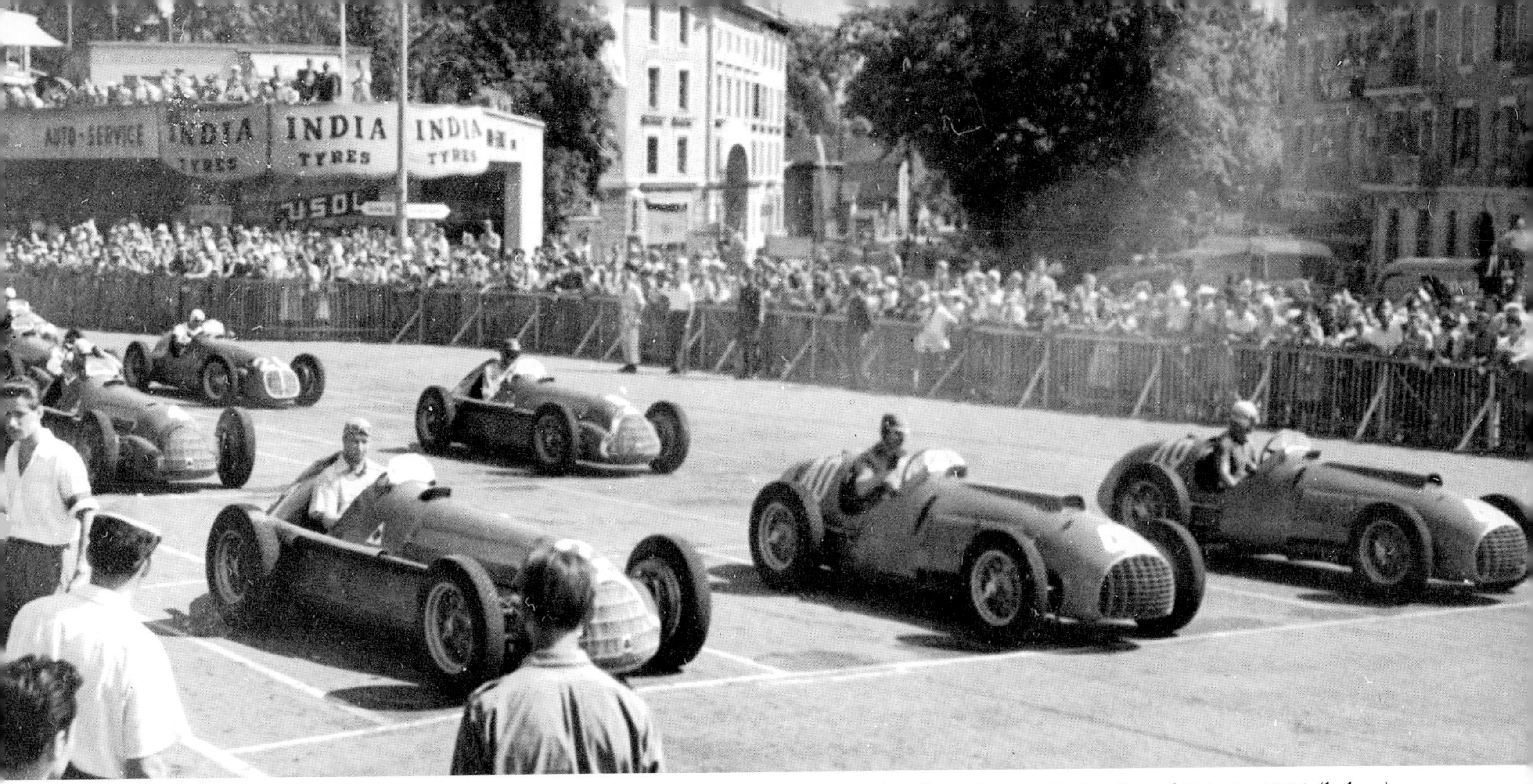

The unsupercharged V12 Ferraris thrust themselves to the front of the grid at the 1950 Geneva Grand Prix (above), where their retirement helps Fangio win. He leads from flagfall to finish in the wet Swiss Grand Prix in 1951 (below), but must give best to Ferrari at that year's German GP (overleaf), placing second behind Ascari.

MERCEDES-BENZ MERCEDES-BENZ
SHELL X-100 MOTOR OEL
BOSCH
BOSCH
X-100 MOTOR OEL
Mobiloel
Mobiloel
Mobiloel
Mobiloel
Englebert-Reifen

FORD
FORD
FORD
FORD
FORD
FORD
DUNLOP

The spirit of Fangio's Alfa years is well portrayed by his enthusiastic push-starters in 1950 (left and opposite), his byplay with a begoggled Farina after the 1950 French GP (Fagioli and Alessio just above the bottle), his congratulations to a Coke-drinking Ascari after the '51 German GP, and his posing between Farina (right) and Fagioli with Froilán González having a look-in.

DE
12
8

At Monte Carlo in 1950 Fangio and Farina rocket away from their front-row starting slots, the Argentine gaining the advantage on the first lap. On his second lap Fangio bursts out of the tunnel into the sunlight and along the quay toward the sharp left at the tobacconist's shop. Glancing up at the crowd overlooking the quay the race leader notices something odd: they aren't looking at him! His thoughts flash back to a day earlier when he was looking through a photo album at the Monaco Auto Club. He saw pictures of the 1936 race in which some cars skidded and crashed on just the quay he is now approaching at 100 miles per hour.

Fangio brakes hard to a stop before the left turn. Around it, previously hidden from his view by the balustrades, are nine crashed Grand Prix cars. On his first lap Nino Farina skidded on a freshly wetted surface and eight others following him crashed into him and each other, fortunately without great personal injury. The road is blocked, but Juan spots a chance. If one car can be moved he can get by. He drives up to it and pushes its tyre by hand, rolling it enough to clear space for his Alfa. From that manoeuvre it is a clear run to a victorious finish.

8
8

That Juan Manuel Fangio knows the shortest way around a circuit is evident from the absolute confidence and precision with which he carves the apex of a turn. He does it at Reims in 1951 (preceding pages), Monte Carlo in 1950 (above), the 'Ring in 1951 (below), and with the bulkier-looking Type 159 Alfa at Monza in 1951. At Silverstone in '51 T. C. March catches him in the full-blooded power-on drift at which he excels. He does it identically lap after lap in his vain chase of González.

In the cliff-hanger that is the 1951 world championship season Juan Fangio benefits from Ferrari's tyre troubles to score a great win on the streets of Barcelona. He climbs the grade at the end of the stately $1^{1}/_{2}$-mile-long Avenida del Generalissimo Franco (preceding pages), counter-steers through the right turn at its end and takes the chequered flag to confirm his first drivers' championship. Among the crowd of well-wishers – as Alessio congratulates Fangio – is Leica-wielding Rudy Mailander, just at the nose of the car.

32
32

CHAPTER 4

Doubts and disasters

'Even for a world champion, it is not easy to take a quick decision when he discovers that he is out of work. Obviously I knew that several makes would offer me their cars to drive. The problem was to decide which of the European manufacturers would give me the best chance of winning.'

Thus did the new champion driver, Juan Manuel Fangio, face the 1952 season. Although Alfa Romeo dithered over it, as it was wont to do, the decision was finally and irrevocably reached that it would retire the magnificent Alfettas after the 1951 season, even though the Formula to which they were racing had two more years to run.

Ascari and his friend and mentor Gigi Villoresi were unshakeably linked with Ferrari for 1952. Ferrari's third regular seat was filled by an Alfa refugee, Nino Farina. In spite of his 1951 exploits Froilán González was not asked back by Ferrari; he and Fangio had ideas of pairing up profitably with suitable teams in the 1952 season. Working as partners rather than rivals, the two Argentines would have a lot to offer. But which team would they favour?

For the increasingly popular Formula 2 races for 2-litre cars Gordini was one possibility; Fangio had a soft spot for the resourceful Frenchman. But 'The Sorcerer' Amédée already had two young, keen, light and cheap drivers in Jean Behra and Robert Manzon. The clear choice was Maserati.

In 1947 the Maserati brothers had left the firm bearing their name, which since 1937 had been owned by the interests of Adolfo Orsi and his son Omer. During that decade Maserati had existed chiefly to design, build and sell racing cars to private teams and drivers. Now, for Formula 2, Maserati was planning to step up to the Ferrari challenge not only by building cars for sale but also by entering works cars.

Juan Fangio had always dealt with the Orsis father and son. They were his interlocutors in 1948 when he

The last Grand Prix car to have a live rear axle, the A6GCM Maserati of 1953 requires alert piloting as Juan Fangio demonstrates with vigorous counter-steering during practice for the Swiss GP. 'The Maserati didn't handle,' recalled champion motorcycle racer Geoff Duke, 'and it was most interesting to watch the Old Man working himself up to getting it through there flat out. I'd watch Fangio – no one else – because he was an absolute maestro.'

first negotiated to buy the 4CLT/48 Formula 1 cars. They had helped him keep the Achille Varzi team Maseratis going. When they told him that they were building a new Formula 2 car for 1952, Fangio agreed to drive it as soon as it was ready. Froilán González put up his hand as well.

Formula 1 was a different story. With Alfa gone and Ferrari fully booked, the options were few. There were rumours about a return to racing by Mercedes-Benz, but that company had put its plans on ice after witnessing the titanic battle between Alfa Romeo and Ferrari at the 'Ring in 1951. Instead it would plan toward the new Formula 1 coming in 1954.

The only major option was an intriguing one: the British Racing Motor, BRM. While battling with González at Silverstone in 1951 Fangio had seen the two low, light-green cars soldiering to finishes in fifth and seventh, split by Sanesi's Alfetta. At the Italian Grand Prix Reg Parnell had put his BRM on the second row of the grid, faster than de Graffenried's Type 159, before it was withdrawn. Its ear-splitting exhaust note and complex V16 engine had made a good impression. With Alfa gone, the BRM looked to be the only car capable of challenging the V12 Ferraris.

'As early as January 1952,' recalled BRM engineer Tony Rudd for Doug Nye, 'while Alfa Romeo dithered over whether or not to withdraw finally from Formula 1, Fangio was actively looking for another berth.' Not surprisingly, BRM was looking in Fangio's direction at the same time. It made contact with him through none other than Eric Forrest Greene, winner of the 500 miles of Rafaela in 1928. Greene had carried on racing in Argentina and added importation of Rolls-Royce and Aston Martin cars to his portfolio.

Related Nye in his BRM history, 'Greene suggested that Fangio should be offered 50 per cent of the starting and prize money, either full travelling and living expenses or a fixed expenses payment each month, plus a small retainer fee, which "would help negotiations as Alfa Romeo had never done anything in this respect" apart from giving him a new road car.' Greene made it clear that González would be part of the package as well. 'After some negotiations,' wrote BRM head Raymond Mays, 'Fangio agreed to fly to Britain and test the car. I felt that to have Fangio test it, even if he did not sign up, would be valuable; if he could not drive it, nobody could.'

Meanwhile two BRMs were being tested at Monza by Stirling Moss and British hillclimb champion Ken Wharton. Fangio told Greene he was wary of trying the car there, only a few kilometres away from his old Alfa Romeo stamping grounds. If Alfa did make a comeback he wanted to be part of its plans; testing a British rival under its nose would not be the best way to keep its friendship.

BRM filed preliminary entries for the first Formula 1 race of 1952, held in Turin's Valentino Park on 6 April, for Fangio, Moss and Wharton. Starting money of £1,500 was offered for one of them, so the team at Monza set about preparing a single BRM for Moss to race. Accompanied by Greenes senior and junior and Argentine Club officials, Fangio and González arrived in Europe in time to be in Turin to see how their potential ride, the BRM, fared against the latest Ferraris in this non-championship race. They were dumbfounded to find no sign of the British car. The most notorious no-show in modern Grand Prix history had done it again.

Bizarrely, Raymond Mays had defied the Turin Auto Club and overruled his chief engineer, his team and an irate Stirling Moss to order the best BRM back to its home base at Bourne in Lincolnshire so that Fangio and González could test it. So eager was Mays to engage the Argentines that he overlooked the fact that BRM was their only option if they wished to continue at the top level of Formula 1. Mays had more bargaining power than he seemed to realise.

On 8 April at a wet Silverstone the two Argentines tried a BRM for the first time. Until then, Raymond Mays wrote, 'every driver who had handled the BRM had treated it with some measure of respect. Some drivers had plainly been scared by its high speed and high engine revolutions; all had been wary of it. Fangio was the first man who was complete master of it. He got in the BRM and shot away, straight up to 11,500rpm as though he had driven the car a score of times. Great blades of water were thrown up from each wheel as he explored his way up the straights in a series of tail-slides alternating with lightning corrections.'

Juan Fangio returned the compliment. 'On the straight it was like a wild beast,' he told Roberto Carozzo. 'Twelve thousand revs! You should have heard the way it buzzed along! Anyone who drove it got out of it half deaf. And you had to be the kind that enjoyed gear changes. This had to be done continually, to ensure that the engine speed did not fall below 7,000 revs. That was the point at which you could call on its real power.'

He asked for a higher seating position to give better visibility and had another request as well: 'One of the first things I said to Mays and the British technicians was that they would have to fit air vents to ventilate the cockpit, otherwise the driver's legs would roast.' In fact Parnell and Peter Walker had roasted at Silverstone in '51. By May, with these changes, Fangio was lapping BRM's private test track a stunning 10 seconds faster than any other driver had managed.

Soon thereafter, said Raymond Mays, 'Juan Perón, President of Argentina, who had taken a personal interest in the negotiations with Fangio and González, wrote to me: "Your decision to enter into negotiations with, and engage our drivers Fangio and González, has pleased me very much and I hope they will bring you success."' BRM was now all dressed up – but with few places to go.

BRM's failure to start at Turin had been the last straw for Europe's race organisers. The race had seen the first non-Ferrari in sixth place, five laps behind the winner. More such contests would not create much in the way of a spectacle. Like a row of dominoes the European auto clubs one after another converted their major fixtures to Formula 2. This became the basis for the drivers' world championship in 1952 and '53 as well. BRM had helped to neuter the Formula 1 for which its cars had been designed.

Early in May Fangio kept faith with Alfa Romeo by driving one of its new 1900 saloons in the Mille Miglia, but it let him down. His first race date with the BRM was on 1 June at Albi in France, the scene of one of his 1949 victories. The V16s qualified first and second but were in dire trouble with head stud problems and retired. Six days later they had to be rebuilt and in running order for a race on Northern Ireland's Dundrod road circuit. There Fangio and Moss missed most of practice so were relegated to the back of the grid and push-started when their engines stalled. Stirling was out early but Fangio lasted longer, lying third when stopped by a clogged fuel filter.

Juan Fangio now had some travelling to do. He was due on the grid at Monza the following afternoon, Sunday, for the Monza Formula 2 GP. There, at last, the new 2-litre Maserati racing car was ready and Fangio was determined to be at its wheel: 'Though I had signed no paper to the effect that I would drive the machine at its début, I had given my word to Omer Orsi of Maserati, and that was more binding than any piece of paper.'

He had planned to fly out in the private plane of Prince Bira, but after retiring early Bira rather inconsiderately had taken wing. With Louis Rosier, Juan caught a flight to London. After finding no flights to Milan they hopped to Paris, where they found that bad weather had wiped out all flights to Italy. Rosier collected his Renault Fregate at the airport and they drove south to Lyon, near his home. Finding no flights there either, Rosier loaned the Fregate to Fangio for the drive over the Mont Cenis Pass to Milan.

Juan arrived at the track in time for a quick shower and change. Although he had not practised – and in fact had never driven the new Maserati – he was allowed to start from the back of the grid. Carving through the 29 starters he was seventh on the first lap, getting the feel of the new twin-cam six. On the second lap, taking his usual tight line, Fangio grazed a low barrier on the inside of the second Lesmo turn. Fatigued, reacting slowly, he failed to catch the resulting slide and shot off the outside of the turn, where an ancient haybale caught and upended his red car. He was thrown out.

'I can remember it all so clearly,' he told Nigel Roebuck, 'going off the road, hitting the bank, taking off and turning over in the air, seeing the trees rushing towards me, being thrown out of the cockpit and landing on a patch of soft grass. I can recall the strong smell of grass just before I passed out. I was wearing a crash helmet – as required by the new regulations that year – and I later found it had a big scrape across one side and the peak was damaged. It had clearly saved my life.'

As for the damage to Fangio, it was assessed after six

days in traction in the Monza Hospital. The doctors diagnosed concussion, possible lesions to the cervical vertebrae and an old neck lesion from a crash suffered in South America. They held his neck and torso immobile in a plaster cast through the rest of June, July and August. It came off on 3 September, in time for him to wave the starting flag for the Italian Grand Prix.

Fangio's hospital visitors were many. He vaguely remembered a driver bringing him a laurel wreath. Americans Briggs Cunningham and John Fitch paid their respects. In July he received Giuseppe Busso, one of the leading Alfa Romeo engineers. Busso unrolled a portfolio of sketches of a new Grand Prix Alfa, the Type 160, he hoped to create for the 1954 Formula 1. He showed Fangio its four-wheel drive, flat-12 engine and radical rearward driving position. 'After a detailed discussion,' said Busso, 'I got his full and enthusiastic approval.'

Back in Buenos Aires at the end of 1952 Fangio went out to the Autodromo to see what was afoot. Juan Gálvez was there with the old 3.8-litre Grand Prix Alfa Romeo that his brother had driven so well. 'I still could not turn my head completely,' Fangio said. Yet he felt it was time to check his competence. 'I climbed into the cockpit with extreme care, as though it were mined. I pulled on my crash helmet, put on my goggles. I wriggled my fingers before my eyes. Good. I could see clearly. I was still myself, otherwise fear would have paralysed me.'

It went well. On the track he found that he was still Juan Manuel Fangio. Returning to the pits, 'Juan Gálvez put on an Olympian look of indifference when I stopped before him. With a detached air he said, "Still goes all right, doesn't it?", as though the trial had been for the car and not for me. In the racing world there are some things one feels but doesn't say. Before I left, Juan Gálvez and I shook hands, a handshake so long and so strong that it hurt us both a bit.'

For Juan Fangio the next season, 1953, was a wild kaleidoscope of dramatic events. His first race back in Europe, in late April, was the Mille Miglia. He came home to Alfa Romeo, which had built a magnificent new 3.6-litre sports-racing coupé, the 6C3000CM, with a chassis as good as its powerful six-cylinder twin-cam engine. Accompanied by Giulio Sala, Fangio was second at the Rome half-way point and ahead of Marzotto's 4.1-litre Ferrari. This looked like a chance to win a race he particularly wanted to add to his collection.

In the mountains between Florence and Bologna, however, the Alfa suddenly stopped answering its helm. Fangio and Sala lifted the bonnet and found, as Juan said, 'that the chassis itself had broken just where the steering box was mounted, and as I wound the steering from lock to lock so the broken support too moved around and allowed the steering box to "think for itself"! I found that when I steered to the left it went where I wanted, but when I steered to the right it would only really go straight on. So I drove on, keeping well down to the right of the road camber where I had the best chance of getting round the right-handed corners.'

At the Alfa pits in Bologna they asked if welding equipment was available but were told it wasn't. 'I went along braking with the gears alone,' Fangio recalled, 'so that only the rear end of the car would slow it down. Bridges were the most dangerous thing, because I had to take aim on them from a long way back to ensure we met them between the parapets. My mechanic and I sat in grim silence in the car, as we knew that something nasty could happen to us at any time. But "Salita" didn't want to give up any more than I did. I finished the final stretch between Bologna and Brescia at an average of over 100mph.'

Fangio finished in second place a scant 11 minutes behind Giannino Marzotto, many fewer minutes than he had lost while coaxing the Alfa Romeo coupé home. His Alfa failed a piston at Le Mans and was crashed by co-driver Sanesi in the Spa 24 Hours. In September, however, he gave the 6C3000CM its only important race victory at Merano in the Southern Tyrol. It was a minor event, 15 laps of an 11-mile road course, but the opposition was major: Lancia's entire sports-racing team. Obligingly they suffered breakdowns and allowed Juan through to a victory with an open-bodied version of the Alfa.

Juan Fangio also had the chance to drive the Lancia D24 sports-racers he had beaten at Merano. 'The idea that I should race for Lancia was Felice Bonetto's,' Juan told Roberto Carozzo. 'A firm friendship had sprung up between Felice and me following my accident at Monza. He visited me more frequently than any other of my colleagues when I was in hospital, and we got on very well.' They had first teamed up to drive a D24 at the Nürburgring the week before the Merano race but had retired with fuel-pump trouble after taking pole position.

Fangio joined Bonetto, Taruffi and new young Italian lion Eugenio Castellotti to race Lancias in November 1953 in the Carrera Panamericana, better known as the Mexican Road Race. For this open-road event the length of Mexico the D24 was ideal, said Juan: 'The car had a lot of torque and was very agile. The engine was very free-revving. Also it had a very good gearbox. Of all the gearboxes I have used, Lancia's is one of the best, a well-synchronised little box that was a joy to handle.'

Rivals of old, Taruffi and Bonetto pressed for the race lead early while Fangio watched and waited. He would never have wished for what happened: a high-speed crash that killed Bonetto instantly. Fangio: 'When I reached Leôn, a boy came up to my car and told me that Bonetto was dead. It came as an awful shock. It was a most unpleasant experience to be told that a friend had been killed and having to go on racing.' Fangio did continue – all the way to a victorious finish ahead of Taruffi. He had driven solo most of the way but suggested that mechanics be taken on the final stages to secure the win for Lancia. Gino Bronzoni had the honour of accompanying him across the line.

Juan Manuel would drive the Lancias twice more in 1954, at Sebring and in the Tourist Trophy at Dundrod. That gearbox would let him down in the Florida race and he would place second in Ulster after jumping from his own broken car to Piero Taruffi's.

Fangio's 1953 season had also been invigorated by more drives in the incredible BRM V16. Under their new ownership by the Rubery Owen Group, the now dark green BRMs were steadily improving. In minor British events in the autumn the Vandervell-modified 41/2-litre Ferrari was too much for Fangio's BRM, but thanks to the organisers at Albi he could extend it on a real circuit in May against that car with Farina driving and Albert Ascari in a works 41/2-litre V12. González and Wharton were his team-mates.

In the heat at Albi for Formula 1 cars Fangio made a perfect start: 'The BRM was really difficult to get off the line because below around 7,000rpm there seemed to be no power at all but at 7,200rpm there was so much power and torque it was almost unbelievable.' Remembered BRM's Raymond Mays, 'On the long back straight Ascari and Fangio passed and re-passed three times, their wheels in the gutter, and they must have been reaching 180mph on the tree-lined road. Fangio was looking in complete control as they came round the corner by the pits. The big Ferrari was almost touching the tail of the BRM and Ascari was trying desperately hard, and looking very harassed.'

The next lap of ten was no less dramatic. Mays: 'After what seemed like an hour of agonised waiting Fangio shot into view again, on exactly the same line, executing exactly the same flick of the wheel as he entered the bend, looking cucumber cool. As he passed in front of me I saw his relaxed face, his beautiful unruffled movements as he confidently held off Ascari, who was working feverishly in his efforts to keep in the picture.'

Both Ferraris shot their bolts in their efforts to keep up, and Fangio won the heat. Tyre trouble that had affected González in the heat kept Fangio from finishing in the Albi final, but he had done all he could for BRM in one of the greatest days ever enjoyed by this troubled car.

In 1954 Mays received approval from Alfred Neubauer of Mercedes-Benz to invite Fangio to drive the BRM in its shorter, lighter Mark II form in autumn races at Goodwood and Aintree. Juan Manuel came to Folkingham on 13 September to test the Mark II and drove it flat-out as usual. But he didn't race it. 'This was the last time he drove a BRM,' said Tony Rudd. 'It was a memorable sight, the multiple world champion driving a Mark II when contemporary for the first, last and only time.' Fangio had his own coda to his career with Britain's BRM: 'It was the most fantastic car I ever drove – an incredible challenge in every way.'

In contrast to his BRM, Alfa Romeo and Lancia dramas, Juan Fangio's season with Maserati in Formula 2 was pretty tame – until the end. Although his six-cylinder Maserati as tweaked by Gioachino Colombo had a strong top end, it was out-torqued by the Ferrari four, which had better traction and handling with its de Dion rear end against the Maserati's live axle. Juan picked up second places behind Ascari's Ferrari at Silverstone and the Nürburgring and behind Mike Hawthorn at Reims in a furious neck-and-neck scrap through the last half of a Grand Prix that the Briton won by one solitary second from a Fangio whose first gear had retired at mid-race.

At Spa Maserati had brought a fourth car for popular Belgian driver and Fangio friend Johnny Claes. Unable to get his car down to decent times Claes asked Fangio if he would try it. The Argentine did and promptly lapped at speeds akin to those he had set in his own car. 'But tell me,' Claes asked Fangio afterward, 'how on earth do you do it?' Paul Frère heard the reply: 'Fangio said nothing at first and extricated himself from the cockpit; he then went quietly to sit on the pit counter and, in his broken English, gave his very plain and simple explanation: "Less brakes, and more accelerator."'

In fact it was in Claes's car, which he took over after leading then breaking in the Spa race, that Juan Manuel had a last-lap crash on the Stavelot bend when trying to avoid the parked Maserati of González. His car up-ended and hurled him out over the windscreen into a ditch. He was lucky to suffer no more than bruising of his face, arms and one side of his body.

It was the turn of others to have last-lap predicaments in the final championship Grand Prix of 1953 at Monza. After his 1952 crash and his lack of success there since 1949, Fangio 'was beginning to fear that bad luck was keeping me from putting up good performances at Monza, and in fact I had begun to worry about whether it might be just as well not to race any more on that track.' But race he did against Ascari, Farina and young Argentine protégé Onofre Marimon in another Maserati in an epic 312-mile battle. After Marimon pitted for repairs he resumed the same pace although several laps back.

The last turn of the last lap told the story. Fangio: 'Ascari, who stood between me and the victory I needed so badly, took the final curve very sharply and his Ferrari did a half spin. He was hit by Marimon. Farina, whom I had only just overtaken and was breathing down my neck, had to swerve to avoid hitting them. In that split second of danger I was through, winning literally in the 312th mile of a 312-mile race. There was such confusion when we crossed the line that the man didn't put down the chequered flag, so I did another lap with Farina behind me, but all the time I thought they had made a mistake. They say I was almost hysterical that day, and I'm not surprised, although as a rule I'm usually rather calm.'

The win secured for Fangio second place in the world championship behind Ascari and just ahead of Farina. It also prompted him to reflect on the nature of his profession: 'Often since that tense and ruthless battle with Ascari, Farina and Marimon I have realised that a motor racing driver may have all the skills – an iron will and nerves of steel – but if he does not have luck he will not win races.' In these troubled seasons Fangio had made heavy demands on his luck and found it sufficient.

Berne's demanding road course is made to order to display the skills of Alberto Ascari, leading, and Fangio almost alongside after the start of the 1953 Swiss Grand Prix. These great rivals are chased by Mike Hawthorn's Ferrari and, behind him, Maserati-mounted Onofre Marimon.

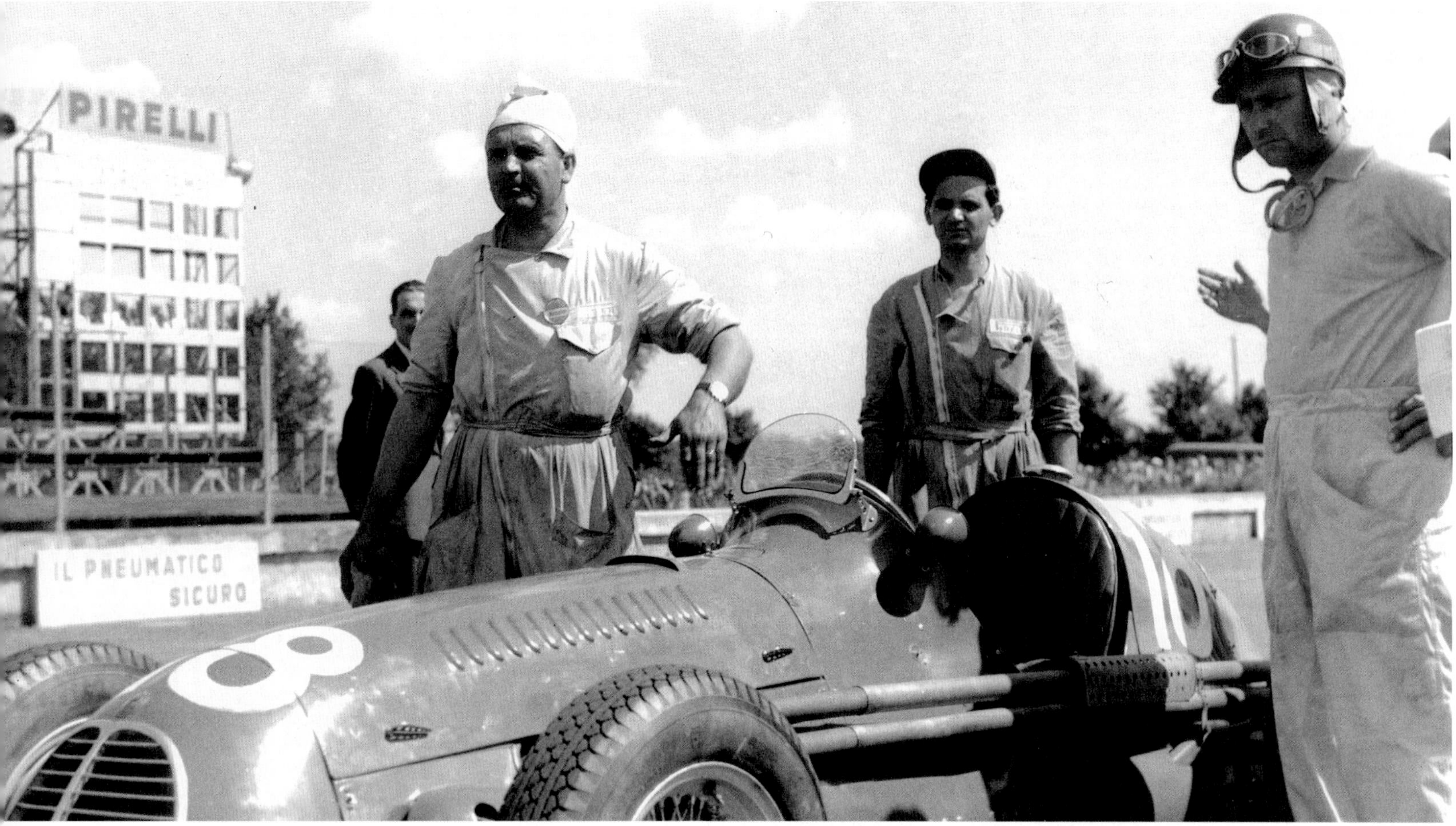
PIRELLI
IL PNEUMATICO
SICURO

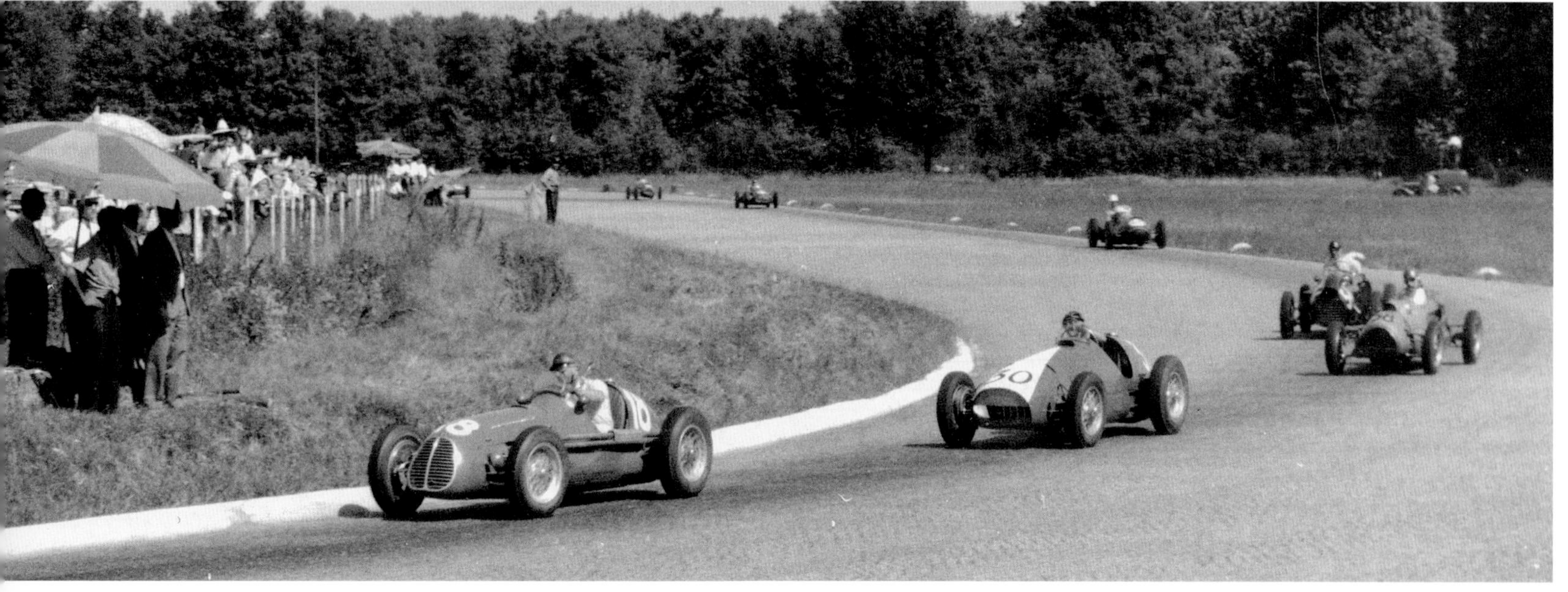

The events of 8 June 1952 hold little joy for J. M. Fangio. Deeply fatigued, he waits for the start of the Monza Grand Prix at the back of the grid with a scalp-protected Guerrino Bertocchi and a Maserati he has never driven. After the first lap he is already seventh ahead of Rudi Fischer's Ferrari, but the next lap ends in disaster when his Maserati crashes and he is thrown out. By September he is fit enough to act as starter for the Italian Grand Prix – but still reluctant to test his neck by turning his head too far.

At Goodwood on 14 April 1952, recalls John Cooper, 'Fangio was due to drive one of those temperamental, over-complicated and ill-fated 16-cylinder BRMs, but as usual the car wasn't ready and didn't even show up. Fangio expressed great interest in our cars, though. I therefore asked him if he would like to try my car and he readily agreed to do a few practice laps. He came in smiling and I then offered him the car for the [Chichester Cup] race. Fangio was delighted, but unfortunately this was the original prototype on which we had done all the testing and the engine went sour during the race. Looking back, however, I must be the only manufacturer who ever had Fangio driving for him with no starting money!' Juan finishes sixth; the other Cooper drivers pictured are Alan Brown (left) and Eric Brandon.

No cars leave a more lasting impression on Juan Fangio than the supercharged 1½-litre V16 BRM, which he races in 1952 and 1953, relishing its seemingly limitless power. He shows its speed at Goodwood in West Sussex in September 1953 (opposite and overleaf) but its chronic unreliability lets him down.

Fangio maintains his Alfa Romeo relationship with drives in the new six-cylinder Alfa sports-racer in 1953. In the Mille Miglia, which he should have won, he finishes second – with empathy from his fans and friends – in spite of wonky steering on the final stages of the open-road race.

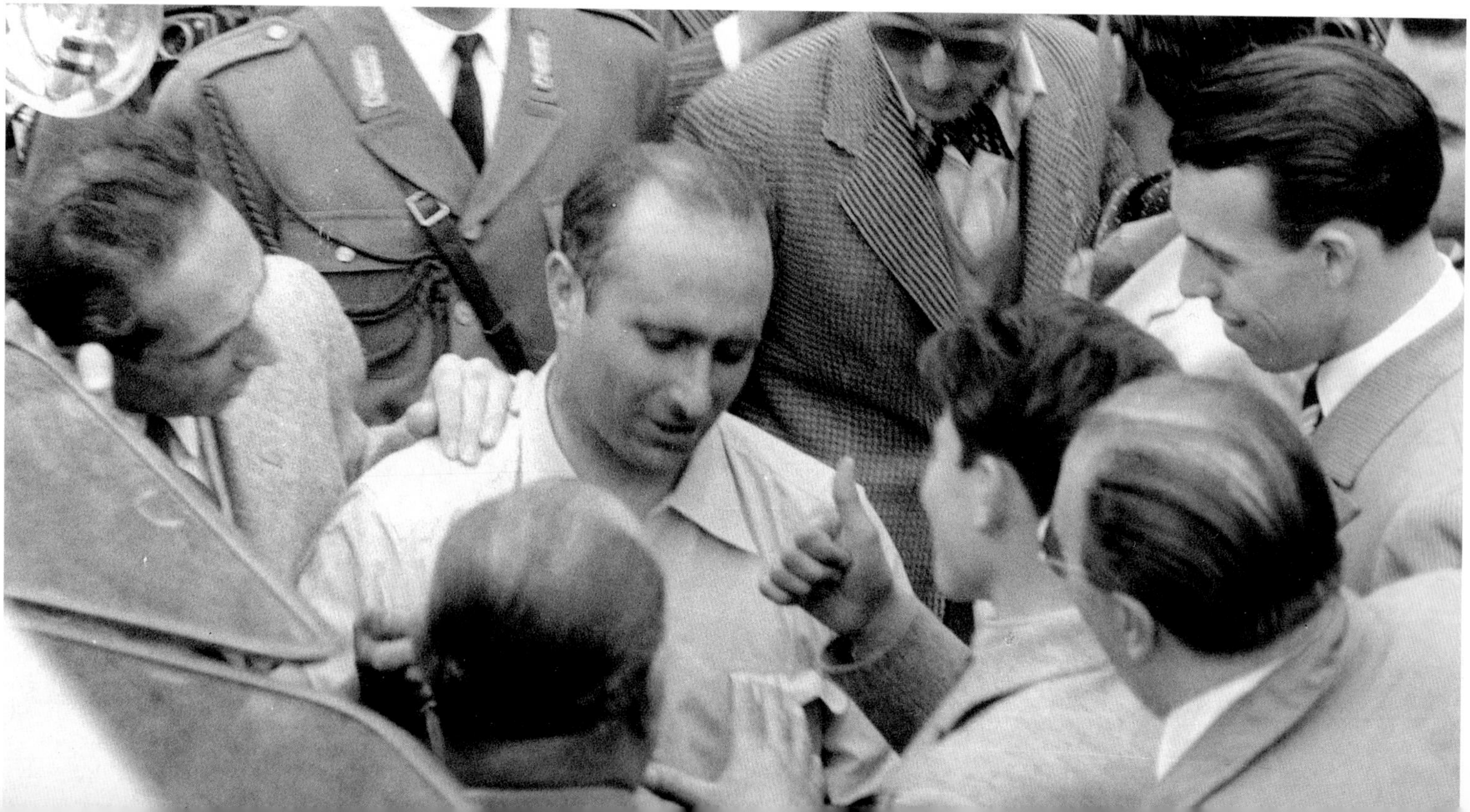

Piston trouble stops the Alfas at Le Mans in 1953 (above left) but Fangio, here with Guidotti and Zanardi, wins at Merano in an open version of the car (above right). He helps Alfa publicise its new 1900 saloon by racing it to 22nd in the 1952 Mille Miglia (below left) and joins the Lancia team (below right) to win the Carrera Panamericana at the end of 1953. Left to right are Taruffi, Bonetto – who will not survive the race – Castellotti, Fangio and Giovanni Bracco.

Braking hard at Berne in 1953 (above), Fangio is unhappy with his car and will take over Bonetto's lower-geared A6GCM and race it from ninth to fourth at the finish. At the 'Ring that year he finishes more than half a minute ahead of Hawthorn, who is chasing him here (below), but can do nothing about Farina's winning Ferrari.

Surviving a hair-raising slipstreaming battle – here leading Farina, Ascari and Marimon – Juan Fangio manages to sneak through a last-lap tangle among his rivals to win the 1953 Italian Grand Prix. 'The race was pretty terrific. Every one of the 80 laps was another fight, another duel with Ascari and Farina, who were close up with me, and almost every lap we changed places for the lead.' He takes an extra lap just to be sure he has really received the chequered flag. Like their driver, the Maserati men are jubilant at this fairytale ending to a difficult season, even chairing the winner in front of the Monza crowd (overleaf).

BP ENERGOL
BP ENERGOL
BP ENERGOL
BP
32

At Silverstone on 13 May 1950 Juan Fangio drives for Alfa Romeo in the first-ever world championship Grand Prix (above). His Type 158 suffers a rare engine failure that day. At Monte Carlo in 1957 Fangio tries valiantly in practice to extract good lap times from the V12-powered 250F Maserati (below), but uses the normal six-cylinder model for the race (preceding page), which he wins.

Reliability is a strong suit of the Mercedes-Benz W196, but not even Fangio can win with it all the time. He places third in the Spanish Grand Prix of 1954 at Barcelona (above) and second in the 1955 British Grand Prix at Aintree (below), just behind winner Stirling Moss in a similar car.

At Silverstone in 1954 Louis Klementaski captures (above, left to right) Karl Kling, Alfred Neubauer and Juan Fangio in a final pre-race huddle. It is not a good day for Mercedes: Fangio is fourth and Kling seventh. At the same venue in August 1950 Guy Griffiths finds (opposite top, left to right) Alberto Ascari, Dorino Serafini, Fangio and Domingo Marimon (father of Onofre) in conversation. Larry Crane is on hand at Long Beach in 1976 (opposite bottom) when a yellow-shirted Fangio listens to blazer-wearing racing driver René Dreyfus after the vintage exhibition race. Attentive to René from left to right are Jack Brabham, Stirling Moss, Innes Ireland, Richie Ginther, Phil Hill, Dan Gurney, Carroll Shelby and Maurice Trintignant. In all nine world championships are represented.

In the 1956 Monaco GP Juan Fangio is trailing Stirling Moss on lap 2 in his Lancia-Ferrari and leading Eugenio Castellotti in an earlier version of this car. Harry Schell will shortly crash his Vanwall (here third) and retire while Fangio places second in the Ferrari of Peter Collins.

Fangio and Castellotti team up on 27 May 1956 to place second in the 1000 Kilometres of the Nürburgring in their Ferrari Monza 860. Fangio earns his keep with Ferrari by driving in seven sports-car races for the Maranello team that season.

The Maserati 250F in its refined 1957 form is the ideal workplace for Juan Manuel Fangio. Its balance and flexibility perfectly suit his style. He is seen winning with it in Germany (above and preceding pages) and at Monaco (below). He retires in the British Grand Prix at Aintree (opposite top) and places second behind the Vanwall of Stirling Moss on the long Pescara road course (opposite bottom).

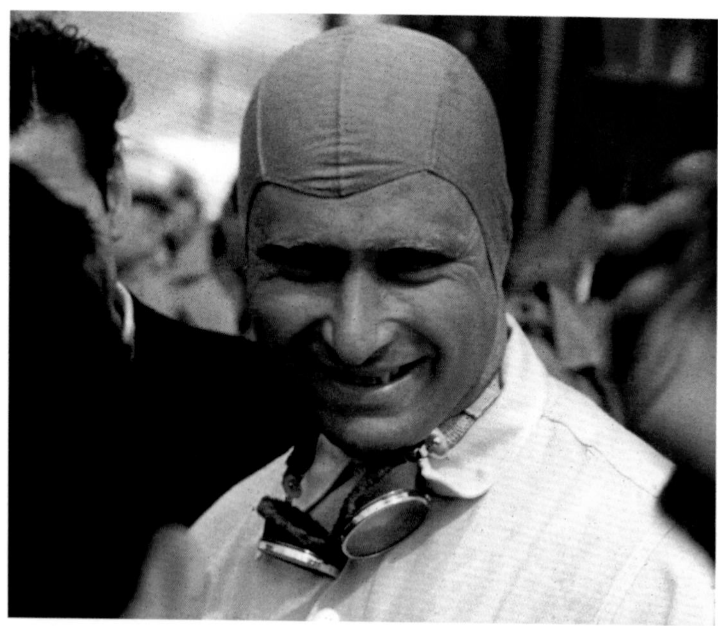

Juan Fangio displays various styles of headgear at Silverstone in 1950 (above left) and at a very warm Berne for the Swiss Grand Prix in 1953 (above right). After his retirement he jokes with Louis Chiron (below) and makes a promotional appearance for Mercedes-Benz at Hockenheim (right) with his old mate and rival Stirling Moss.

Mobil
Mobil
Mobil
OPEL
CAMPARI
MERCEDES

Fangio has passed Peter Collins and is chasing Mike Hawthorn in his spectacular drive to victory in the 1957 German Grand Prix (above). During this dramatic race he pushes his own capabilities and those of the 250F Maserati to the limit (opposite top).

At the finish the crowd at the Nürburgring in 1957 is wildly enthusiastic, having witnessed one of the great drives of motor sports history (below). Fangio confirms his fifth world championship with this win. At Monte Carlo in 1955 (overleaf) Fangio's Mercedes passes fellow Argentine Roberto Mieres in his works 250F Maserati. Fangio retires with an engine failure that sidelines the entire Mercedes-Benz team.

2
2

18

CHAPTER 5

Grand Alliance

Although the Mercedes-Benz racing cars of 1954 and 1955 were superb examples of the application of high technology and tradition to racing, some would suggest that their world championships in those years would not have been achieved without Juan Fangio's skill and indeed artistry. There is some truth in this. In both years Fangio was the undisputed team leader in the silver Formula 1 Mercedes, and whenever the cars from Stuttgart were in a position to win – which was often – Fangio was at the forefront.

Looking back, the combination of Mercedes-Benz and Fangio seems obvious. Of course Mercedes would build great cars and of course they would attract the best driver. Rudy Uhlenhaut of Daimler-Benz put it simply: 'About 50 per cent depends on the car and 50 per cent on the driver. We had a good look round and chose the best – and that was Fangio.' In fact it was a much nearer-run thing.

The brilliant Alfred Neubauer walks a tricky tightrope between his own management at Daimler-Benz and Fangio in Argentina to sign the great driver for 1954. Beginning with the French Grand Prix at Reims in July of that year (preceding pages) their relationship grows into a successful racing partnership.

It might not have been Fangio. Daimler-Benz team manager Alfred Neubauer planned to enter his first post-war Grand Prix season in 1954 with a German driver cadre: pre-war star Hermann Lang, still quick on his day; engineer-racer Karl Kling, who knew the new car inside and out; Fritz Riess, who had been fast in the 300SL; and speedy youngster Hans Herrmann. But Neubauer and his technical boss Fritz Nallinger knew that they needed, as Nallinger put it, a 'master driver' to lead the team and ensure success.

'Master drivers' were not thick on the ground, but some were around. Ascari and his mentor Villoresi had been snapped up by Gianni Lancia for his new Formula 1 effort, expected to bear fruit late in 1954, the first year of the new Formula 1. Nino Farina came into consideration, although the proud Torinese had not been best pleased when Neubauer reneged (in favour of Fangio) on a verbal agreement to sign Farina for his team for Argentina in 1951. Compensation had to be paid.

Of the Britons Mike Hawthorn could enter the frame; his Grand Prix career had leapfrogged that of Stirling

Moss and he had won at Reims in 1953, just edging Fangio. Froilán González was another sparkling new star. But of all these Neubauer had set his cap for Juan Manuel Fangio. 'He knows something about sliding the turns,' he told his colleagues. 'That's our man.'

To his credit Neubauer started angling for the Argentine racer as early as mid-1950. He wanted him for the 1951 *Temporada* in Argentina and later to lead the team of 1½-litre supercharged Grand Prix cars he hoped Daimler-Benz would build. His efforts to attract Fangio to tests at the 'Ring and to a factory visit in the autumn were in vain. Fangio was, however, awarded a Buenos Aires Mercedes dealership that winter – a clear expression of the company's confidence in him. But when the Argentine racer drove the 3-litre Mercedes in the 1951 winter races it did not show its best form, to Neubauer's utter mortification. This was just the opposite of what he needed to lure the cautious Juan Manuel.

The stakes were raised in June 1951 when Daimler-Benz decided to build a fleet of new W165 V8 racers to compete in 1952. Neubauer had to seduce Fangio away from Alfa, deploying 'talents that Casanova would have envied. I had to use all my arts of enticement, pull every trick out of the box to win the confidence of the Argentine, who was as coy as a maiden before her first kiss.'

Just at the end of May Neubauer finally achieved one of his goals: a factory visit by Fangio. Accompanying him were Juan Carlos Guzzi of the Argentine Auto Club, Froilán González and Onofre 'Pinocho' Marimon, the racing-mad son of Domingo Marimon, who had both helped the youthful Juan Manuel and raced against him and the Gálvez brothers. Motoring to Stuttgart in Juan's Alfa Romeo, they toured the famous museum and dined convivially with Neubauer.

Later that week Alfred Neubauer drove to the Nürburgring to watch the Friday practice for the 3 June Eifelrennen, a Formula 2 race at which the Ferraris were expected but failed to show. Leaving the circuit, what to his wondering eyes should appear but a black and red Alfa saloon by the side of the road and, kicking its tyres, Guzzi, Marimon, González and Fangio. The drivers had wanted to take a look at the 'Ring – and they had, initiating Marimon's obsession with the track – but grinding noises from the rear end meant their Alfa wouldn't go much farther.

Thinking quickly, Neubauer said he'd go at once to the Mercedes main dealer at nearby Coblenz and send back a team of mechanics to fix the axle, loaning the Argentines a car in the meantime so they could have dinner and even providing an interpreter. When the mechanics arrived, bringing a bearing that fitted the Alfa, they found that Fangio had already rolled up his sleeves and dismantled the rear axle. They were on their way again that evening, thanks to the gratis intervention of Daimler-Benz.

In July, for the 1951 German Grand Prix, Neubauer made sure Fangio had a good room in the Nürburgring's Sporthotel, a room with the bathtub in which Juan liked to have a good long soak after a tough race. He gave Fangio some of the latest German driving goggles to replace the 'welders' goggles' that he had been using, and when the driver had a bout of conjunctivitis Neubauer arranged for a top physician to attend him.

The relationship seemed to be warming. But when in September Neubauer invited Fangio to the 'Ring for comparative tests of Mercedes-Benz racers (his own drivers couldn't get down to the pre-war sub-10-minute lap times) the Argentine Club's Guzzi pleaded a conflict with the Paris Salon. Fangio, we may be sure, was wary of upsetting Alfa, with whom he was on the brink of winning his first world championship.

The pressure on Neubauer lessened in the autumn when Daimler-Benz decided not to build new 1½-litre cars after all but instead to plan ahead to the new Formula 1 for 1954. His German driver squad was adequate for his 300SL racers in 1952, the year of Fangio's injury; the only non-German to race those cars was American John Fitch. In 1953, however, with Fangio now racing happily albeit unsuccessfully for Maserati, which had an impressive new car on the stocks for 1954, Alfred Neubauer had to get busy again.

Maserati *patron* Adolfo Orsi deeply desired to retain the services of Fangio for 1954, now that his company had adjusted to the idea of running a works Formula 1 team. In fact Fangio would drive Maseratis in the first two 1954 Grands Prix. Another lusting for his skills was young Gianni Lancia, for whom Fangio had just won the Mexican Road Race and was booked for Sebring in '54. He was building a team of Grand Prix cars and asked Fangio to join his strength. Pointing out that Lancia had already signed Ascari and Villoresi, Juan cheekily chided the industrialist by saying that it wouldn't be fair for him to have *all* the best drivers. But in February the Buenos Aires papers were reporting that Juan would race for Lancia.

These teams, skilled, experienced and successful, were serious rivals to Daimler-Benz in Fangio's affections. So was Alfa Romeo, although the radical racing car Busso had shown Fangio at his Monza bedside in 1952 would never be completed. Nor could Ferrari be ruled out. Enzo was in one of his sulks, threatening to abandon racing and retire to a monastery. He told Neubauer that he was free to negotiate with any or all of his drivers. In the autumn of 1953 Neubauer again struck up his tango with the Argentine.

Fresh from two victories on the trot at Monza and Modena in Maseratis, Fangio granted an exceptional favour to Neubauer at the end of September. Daimler-Benz was tyre-testing at Monza with the 1952 300SL and with an extensively modified SL that had some of the features of the 1954 GP car. Fangio agreed to come along and set some bogey times. In the 1952 car he was little faster than Kling, Lang, Riess and Herrmann, but in the modified car he was a clear 2 seconds quicker than they were.

This was Neubauer's opportunity to make his pitch to Fangio – and he did – but he had one hand tied behind his back: he couldn't confirm a racing programme for 1954. The new silver cars were progressing; he hoped to begin the sports-car season with the Mille Miglia at the beginning of May and Grand Prix racing in mid-year at Reims. But he couldn't commit to these dates. He said he wished there was an October Spanish Grand Prix on the '53 calendar because he 'wanted to make a gift of a less cloudy wine' to Fangio by that time. All he could do was ask Fangio not to make any firm commitment to another team for the 1954 season.

Making firm commitments too early for '54 was the last thing on Juan Manuel's mind when he returned to Argentina in October. Neubauer was able to communicate with this most important of his Buenos Aires dealers through a company director based there, Baron Arnt von Korff. His strong links with the Spanish-speaking countries had found von Korff first in Spain and now in Argentina on the strength of Daimler-Benz. Keenly interested in racing, the Baron was an able and appropriate interlocutor for Fangio. Another ally was the local businessman who headed Mercedes-Benz sales in Argentina, Juan Antonio.

On 27 October Neubauer set out for von Korff the general terms of the proposition he was able to offer Fangio. The driver, he said, would receive all of the starting money and prize money earned by his performance in every race, less a 10 per cent deduction shared among the team members. Neubauer pointed out that normal practice was to pay a driver no more than a third to a half of these amounts, because teams needed the rest of the money to support their racing. Unlike them, Daimler-Benz would underwrite all the costs and give 90 per cent of all race earnings, including those from accessory companies, to Fangio.

Alfred Neubauer's earnest hope that this generous offer – communicated to Fangio by von Korff – would lead to an early commitment by the driver was in vain. Not until 12 January 1954 did the Baron revert to Neubauer with Fangio's comments on the proposed deal. He was ready to sign, said von Korff, but wanted assurances on some points. One was that no other Argentine driver would be signed. 'It is correct,' confided the Baron, 'that there are differences between F. and his countryman G.' Neubauer assured him that he would sign no other non-German drivers, let alone González, adding that there was no truth in the rumours that Mercedes was negotiating with Ascari.

Fangio asked for freedom to race for other teams outside his commitments to Mercedes-Benz. He also said he appreciated the suggestion that Mercedes would reimburse him if it failed to take part in a race, but that it was more important to him in such a situation to be free to get a ride with another team. Von Korff told Neubauer that it was vital that he provide a firm draft contract soon and especially that it specified the race programme.

'Fangio has firmly decided to join with us,' wrote von Korff early in February. 'Contractual matters are far from his thoughts and he has complete confidence that we – eg above all you, Mr Neubauer – will deal with him loyally and correctly. His understanding of formal matters is not great. Fangio thinks that a contract would not be so important, because ours is a serious firm and it would be sufficient to have an agreement such as we have reached between us here; I take a different view and absolutely recommend a clear contract, which I explained to Fangio and to which he agreed.'

On 23 February, a Tuesday, Fangio stopped in at von Korff's offices at Charcas 684, Buenos Aires, for a farewell chat before departing to Florida to race at Sebring. The Mercedes director gave the driver a set of photos of the just-completed envelope-bodied W196 Grand Prix car, which made a positive impression. Nevertheless Fangio pressed von Korff. Why have so many weeks passed with nothing being resolved? Nothing really clarified? Was Mercedes serious or not?

Over their coffees, in this difficult atmosphere, a secretary showed the Baron the morning's mail. It included a letter from Neubauer and a draft contract – in German and unsigned. Realising that it was vital to gain a commitment from the driver before he fell into the clutches of the Lancia team at Sebring, von Korff arranged a rushed translation of the draft and reviewed it with Fangio. The driver then dated and signed its upper left corner with the word *'conforme'* – 'agreed'. For von Korff this was a happy resolution of what had been for him, so far from Stuttgart, a difficult task. 'You can believe,' he wrote to Neubauer, 'that all in all winning Fangio to our side was not so easy.'

On 1 March the veteran racing director unburdened himself to the Baron on the problems he had been experiencing behind the scenes. 'If you and Mr Fangio have been wondering why a pause had seemingly arisen after last year's written preliminary discussions, there were good grounds. In fact there was hesitation on the part of the directors here to commit to a sufficient number of racing cars to secure the participation of Fangio.'

The stumbling block had been the absolute determination of technical director Fritz Nallinger that Mercedes-Benz should compete in the 1954 Mille Miglia. If this had been given priority, Neubauer explained, it would have been possible to complete only four Grand Prix cars – not enough to guarantee a start for Fangio in all six of the remaining championship races including Reims. 'Matters had almost reached the point that we were considering distancing ourselves from a contract with Fangio,' wrote Neubauer, 'because the certainty of his participation was not a given.

'It took weeks for us to be able to convince him,' Neubauer said of Nallinger, 'that we would simply not be ready' for the Mille Miglia. In fact, the sports cars were not ready to compete until the *1955* Mille Miglia. 'All these decisions had to be made,' continued Neubauer, 'and finally fell on the evening of 26 February, whereupon the already prepared contract was signed by the management board. There was really a lot of effort here behind the fashioning of sound support for Fangio.'

The effort on Alfred Neubauer's side, it was clear, was so to emphasise the company's participation in Grand Prix races that it would be possible to engage Fangio to lead the team. He prevailed against Nallinger's desire to attack across a broad front of both sports and racing cars, which would have risked the company's Formula 1 effort to such an extent that – in Neubauer's view – Daimler-Benz would not have been justified in asking the great Argentine to drive its cars.

Sports-car races in 1954 (Le Mans, the 'Ring and Mexico) were still foreseen in the final contract for the season, which Fangio did not sign until 30 March. In addition to the generous terms of the draft contract it assured the driver of a dollar-value fee for starting in those races, such as Le Mans and Mexico, that did not pay starting money. If Mercedes failed to start a contracted race Fangio had the choice of a compensatory fee or his freedom to drive for another team.

According to a daily allocation Juan Fangio's expenses were paid while he was in Europe. Although the contract didn't mention it, at the driver's request the expenses of his lady friend Beba were covered as well. In the case of 'Mrs Fangio', as she was called, this was warmly agreed to by the board and himself, Neubauer said: 'We have always had the experience that especially in case of accidents the women are very necessary, because they are the only ones who take care of the injured when the racing team has to up stakes and depart.'

The contract provided for substantial amounts to be paid in the event of hospitalisation, disablement or death. It assured Fangio that no other Argentine driver would be engaged by the team in 1954. A loan car was to be provided, either a 220 or a 300. In fact, after urgings from the Argentine side that nothing less than a top-of-the-range 300S would suit Fangio's prestige in the eyes of his countrymen, one of these costly custom-built cars was made available.

The car that counted, of course, was the W196 Grand Prix racer with its straight-eight engine. Fangio saw it for the first time on the Monday after his 20 June victory in the Belgian Grand Prix. He and the rest of the team were at Reims for two days of tests three weeks before the car's first race. 'From the very first test,' he wrote, 'I was sure that I had in my hands the perfect car, the sensational machine that drivers dream about all their lives. I had not the least doubt about the race result: a Mercedes would be first across the finishing line. Throughout the entire race the two silver cars driven by Kling and myself went perfectly, almost in unison. I led Kling across the line by a wheel.'

Their debut victory in the French Grand Prix 40 years after Mercedes's 1914 success in the same race was storybook stuff for the sleek silver cars. In practice Fangio won 50 bottles of Reims champagne with the first-ever lap at over 200kph. But the team knew they still had a lot to do. 'That first year we had a car that was a bit heavy and it was very difficult to win on a small circuit,' said Fangio. He was critical of the braking, which was improved for 1955. Continental's tyres were not yet up to Pirelli standards as a wet race at Silverstone showed: Fangio could do no better than fourth, a lap behind winner González/Ferrari. Third ahead of him was 'Pinocho' Marimon, now leading the Maserati team.

Mercedes with open-wheeled bodies were finally ready for the second day of practice for the German Grand Prix. There the Maserati team took Stirling Moss officially under its wing, which Marimon interpreted as a challenge. Pressing hard just before the bridge at Wehrseifen his Maserati locked a wheel and shot through a hedge and down a slope to a crashing halt.

'Between the two "great Argentines" there were major tensions then,' Hans Herrmann recalled of the Fangio/González relationship. 'I don't know the reasons, but I know very well that they kept out of each other's way as much as possible and scarcely exchanged a word. But when the report of the accident reached the pits the two men fell sobbing in each other's arms: *"Es muerto"*, "He's dead."' The two racers immediately drove the six miles to the scene.

'Together we ran to where Marimon was lying,' wrote Fangio. 'He was already dead, his chest terribly crushed by the steering wheel. He was surrounded by a group of German spectators who had extricated him from the wreckage of his car and were now standing helplessly by in shocked sympathy while a priest, who had apparently materialised from nowhere, was reciting a prayer in Latin. I remember now that his Latin with its strong German accent sounded strange to my ears for he was reciting the same prayer I had learned as a choirboy in our little church at Balcarce.'

'Fangio was so shaken,' said team-mate Herrmann, 'that he didn't want to start the race. It required all the persuasive artistry of Neubauer to change his mind.' But start he did, from pole. Yet in the more agile Ferrari González had a commanding lead when the cars emerged from the twistiest part of the course to attack the straighter final four kilometres. It seemed almost impossible for Fangio to catch González – yet he did.

'In fact only Fangio would have been able to carry out such a difficult task,' wrote Corrado Millanta, 'to overtake González in the last fast turn in a slight downhill just before the stands, where everyone else was very careful. You arrive here at maximum speed after a two-kilometre straight to a turn that appeared abruptly after the road's camber hid it until the last second. This extremely difficult manoeuvre, which would have demanded calm and tranquillity, was carried out when the corpse of the poor Pinocho, so loved by Fangio, was still at the small hospital at Adenau and when inexorably appeared, on every lap, downhill at the beginning of that dangerous turn, the horrid rent in the hedge caused by Pinocho's car before he hurtled down into empty space.'

Fangio was never headed in the next race at Berne. At Monza in September he had a lucky victory when Moss's leading Maserati sprung an oil leak. At Barcelona in October neither the all-enveloping nor the open-wheeled Mercedes suited the course. Fangio nursed his open-wheeled car to a third-place finish, good enough to confirm his second world championship. The Mercedes boffins set to making better cars for 1955. Fangio: 'After they modified it, the car won everywhere, a very difficult car to break. It was an incredible car.'

Conditions for their star driver were improved as well. In December directors Nallinger and Jakob wrote to Juan Manuel suggesting a three-month extension of his 1954 contract while they sorted out the 1955 arrangements. They also broke the delicate news of the engagement of Stirling Moss to strengthen the team, 'because in the event of a retirement of yourself we would cut too poor a figure in relation to our substantial commitment. Moreover Mr Moss is an avowed partisan of yourself and we certainly believe that the relationship between you will be, and remain, good.' Baron von Korff was rewarded for his efforts in Buenos Aires with a new position for 1955: assistant to Alfred Neubauer.

Fangio's new contract, signed on 14 April and taking effect from the Mille Miglia on 1 May, introduced a guaranteed level of payment for each Grand Prix and each major sports-car race he contested, higher for the latter than the former. If the starting money paid fell short of the guaranteed amount, Daimler-Benz made up the difference. He received a daily compensation for his eight-month stay in Europe, plus full reimbursement of all travel. It was by any standards a generous agreement.

We can assume that some *ex gratia* payments were made to top up Fangio's income for a season in which the French, German, Swiss and Spanish Grands Prix were cancelled in the wave of ill-feeling about motor sports that swept the world after the Le Mans disaster. The surviving races were all won by Fangio with the exception of Monaco, where all the silver cars broke, and the British race at Aintree, where Moss was the winner. Juan Manuel suggested in some circles that his car was given a lower axle ratio there to help Moss win, but the *Rennabteilung* (racing department) records show no ratio differences.

In the 300SLR sports car Fangio won at the 'Ring and Sweden's Kristianstad. His second places in the Mille Miglia (single-handed and on seven cylinders), Tourist Trophy and Targa Florio were crucial in winning the sports-car championship for Mercedes-Benz. At Le Mans, after a tense and hard-fought duel with Mike Hawthorn's Jaguar, Fangio was about to lap team-mate Pierre Levegh in front of the pits when the latter clipped Lance Macklin's swerving Austin-Healey and hurtled into the stands, killing himself and more than 80 spectators in the sport's worst-ever disaster.

'I had but one thought,' Fangio recalled. 'How on earth was I going to get through? At the speed at which I was travelling I had to avoid any sudden movement. By some miracle I managed to give a slight flick and squeeze through the debris which was flying between Macklin's car, which was still spinning, and the pits from which Hawthorn was accelerating a few yards further on. After I passed through the crashing cars, without touching anything or anyone, I started to tremble and shake, for at that moment I had been waiting for the blow, holding strongly to the steering wheel. Instead the way had opened and I passed through.'

Bowing to suggestions that to carry on unfeelingly in France would awaken ugly memories of the recent war, Daimler-Benz withdrew its still-healthy cars in the early morning hours. Co-driving with Moss, Fangio had a two-lap lead. Neither driver would ever have a better chance to add a Le Mans victory to their glittering careers.

Exemplifying the care and attention given by Mercedes-Benz to the cars to be driven by Juan Fangio is his seat and control fitting in the new 300SLR sports-racing car at Stuttgart early in 1955. Fangio and Kling (at left) never doubt that the full resources of the company are being placed at their disposal.

Ascari (10) joins Kling and Fangio in the front row for the first appearance of the new Silver Arrows at Reims on 4 July 1954. Before the start Kling is attended by his mechanic Karl Bunz while Fangio's Weber is close at hand as well.

Thanks to supplementary fuel tanks fitted just before the race, the thirsty Mercedes are able to complete the 1954 French Grand Prix non-stop. Their striking aerodynamic bodies make the rest of the field at Reims look decidedly antiquated.

LE CIMENT
TARMACADAM PAR LES

Kling and Fangio are this close (opposite) through most of the race at Reims; in fact Kling thinks he has won but miscounts the final laps. Fangio and his Mercedes face difficult conditions in 1954 at a cold, wet and slippery Silverstone (top), and a hot and dirty Barcelona (bottom).

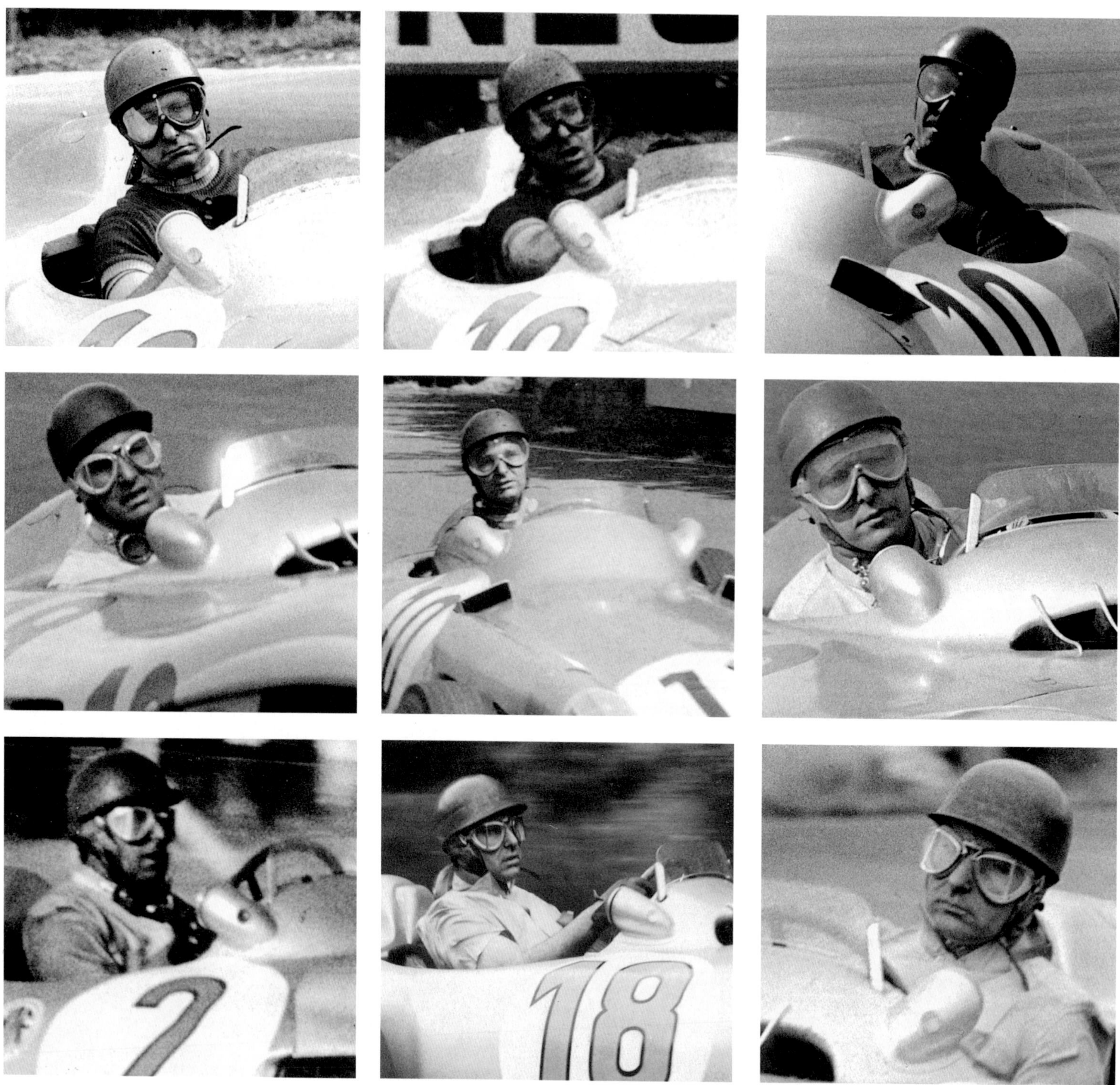

Juan Manuel Fangio respects the performance and staying power of the W196 Mercedes-Benz of 1954 and '55 but never gives the impression that he finds the cars easy or particularly enjoyable to drive. His expressions (above) tell the story, also on his way to victory in the Swiss Grand Prix of 1954 (right) in a shot by a daring Rudy Mailander. Fangio is racing in 1954 (overleaf) at the Nürburgring (top) and at Silverstone (bottom).

4

A hint of the challenging conditions faced in Sicily's Targa Florio is given by scenes at the start (above left) and on the circuit (below left). Fangio's second place there with Karl Kling secures the sports-car championship for Mercedes-Benz in 1955. Fangio's two 1955 outright victories driving the 300SLR are in the Nürburgring's Eifelrennen (above right) and at Sweden's Kristianstad circuit, where he is burning rubber from the Le Mans start. Maddeningly Stirling Moss has, as usual, already departed.

Before the 1955 crash at Le Mans that darkens the skies above the circuit and over Europe's motor sports, Juan Fangio (Mercedes-Benz 19), Mike Hawthorn (Jaguar 6) and Eugenio Castellotti (Ferrari 4) wage a ferocious and awesome battle for the lead. The Mercedes are withdrawn after the crash and Hawthorn (with Ivor Bueb) goes on to victory.

ESSO

What Mike Hawthorn memorably called 'a glittering collection of first class cars and a company of great drivers which we were never again to see assembled together' roars away from the starting grid at Monte Carlo in 1955. Alberto Ascari in the Lancia D50 splits Moss (6) and Fangio (2) in the front row. During the race Fangio and Moss are lapping Louis Chiron in another D50; this is the last Grand Prix for the veteran Chiron who first raced in 1924. Maserati-mounted Cesare Perdisa looks on.

Bankings figure in various ways in Juan's seasons with Mercedes-Benz. The streamlined cars face little opposition on the steep brick banking of Berlin's Avus track in the 1954 Berlin Grand Prix (above); Karl Kling is the winner and Hans Herrmann places third. Fangio tackles the Nürburgring Carousel (below) during practice for the 1954 German Grand Prix.

The spectacular new banked oval built at Monza is included in the track's Grand Prix circuit for the first time in 1955. Fangio (18) wins after Moss (16) retires in the last Grand Prix race contested by the W196 Mercedes-Benz. A chapter in Juan Fangio's life is ending as well.

Among the penalties for Fangio's success in the 1954 Swiss Grand Prix are a hug and a kiss from countryman Froilán Gonzáles (above). His reaction to this experience is telling. He examines other rewards of success, his cups for the 1954 French Grand Prix (below left) and the 1955 Italian Grand Prix (below right) – bookends to his Formula 1 career with Mercedes-Benz.

World champion for the second time after the end of the Spanish Grand Prix in 1954 (above), a weary and dirty Juan Fangio is interviewed by one of the Sojit brothers and accepts a congratulatory bouquet for his second-place finish. After the exhaustingly hot 1955 Argentine Grand Prix (below left) Fangio can barely stand upright for the obligatory congratulations from Juan Perón. His stamina sees him through as well in his struggle to finish fourth in the 1954 British Grand Prix (below right).

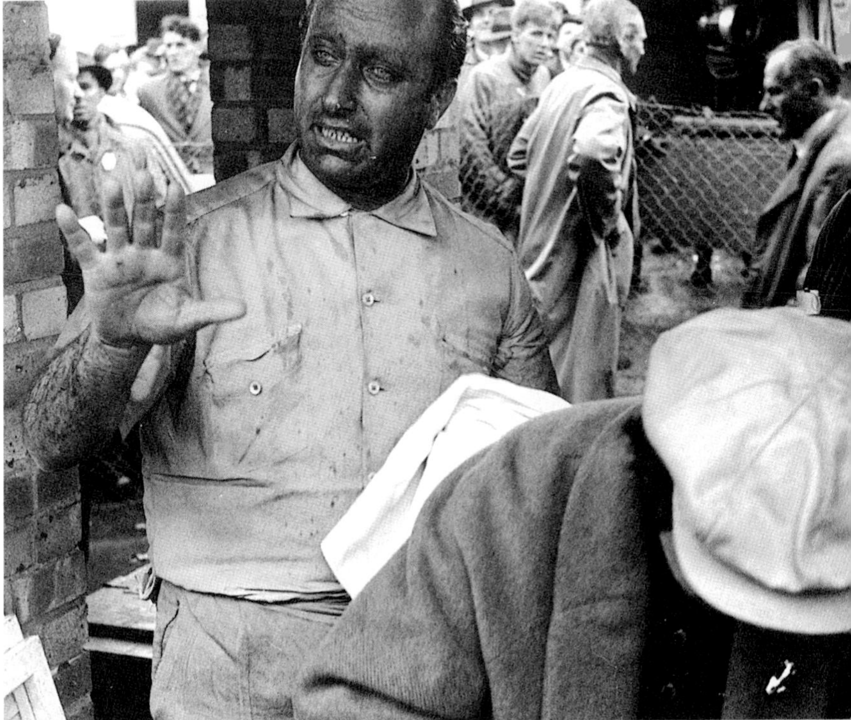

2
ENGLEBERT

CHAPTER 6

In the camp of the enemy

'I must say the year with Ferrari was not happy. I never felt comfortable there. Since I first raced in Europe I had always been in a team that was opposing Ferrari. Now I was joining him.' How had Juan Manuel Fangio, fresh from his second world championship with Mercedes-Benz and third in all, found himself in this situation? Fangio was reputed to be the master at gaining the best position with the best team. Yet here he was in the camp of the enemy, driving for a team that had engaged him out of desperation, not desire.

Racing was, in fact, what Juan Fangio had planned *not* to do in 1956. He had already carried on for five more seasons after his first in 1949, that one year he would race in Europe before returning to his businesses in Argentina. In 1956 he would be 45; eager drivers half his age were nipping at his heels. Moss had already shown in 1955 that he would be a deadly future rival. 'I was going to get out of racing,' Fangio told Roberto Carozzo. 'When Daimler-Benz announced that it was pulling out, I thought the time had come for me as well. I wanted to return to Argentina for good.'

Bernard Cahier rightly focuses on Fangio in the foreground of the front row of the grid for the 1956 German Grand Prix. Juan in a Lancia-Ferrari is on pole just a heartbeat ahead of next man Peter Collins, followed by Castellotti, also in a Lancia-Ferrari, and a Maserati-mounted Moss. Stirling finds him uncatchable that day.

To say that Juan Fangio and Daimler-Benz were parting on good terms would be rank understatement. Company chairman Fritz Könicke wrote to the driver on 23 December to mark the expiration of their second contract. 'At our victory ceremonies,' said Könicke, 'in your brief remarks you made it clear that you had a good appreciation of the decision of our house to have a racing hiatus. We thank you for your great understanding ... Our efforts and commitments have been accompanied by unprecedented success, in that it was possible to win two world championships thanks to your outstanding driving. You will stand for all time in the most glorious position in the history of our house, and we avow to you an immutable trust and friendship, hoping that you will also remain a constant friend.'

In his 12 January reply Fangio said that he had been happy to be allowed to drive for Mercedes and that he felt himself to be a member of 'the Mercedes-Benz family. I would like to take this opportunity,' he added, 'to transmit to all of you, the directors, naturally also the unsurpassable team chief, racing manager Director Neubauer, the engineers, mechanics and workers who all played their part in the beautiful successes that were jointly achieved, my most sincere wishes for a happy new year.'

Juan Fangio the fatalist took these events as a sign. He had just become the first racing driver to win three world championships, surpassing Alberto Ascari's two crowns. His two seasons with Daimler-Benz had rewarded him lavishly; by his standards he was a wealthy man. His business interests in Argentina were well established. 'At the end of 1955,' he said, 'I considered the possibility of retiring for the first time.'

Fangio's first championship in 1951 had coincided with the apogee of the career of another Juan, a man who had strongly encouraged his activities abroad, Juan Domingo Perón. That was the year of his re-election as Argentina's leader, on the arm of the much-adored Evita. But by the end of 1951 Argentina had exhausted her gold reserves and 1952 saw the death of his most fervid and loyal supporter, beloved by her 'shirtless ones', María Eva Duarte Perón. Although Juan Perón had done much to democratise Argentina, his nationalistic approach to its economic problems failed to arrest its decline.

The Catholic church, which had strongly supported Perón at first, excommunicated him in 1954. In September 1955 Perón's fellow military officers presented him with an ultimatum: either resign or there would be a civil war. Perón chose the former. He left Argentina, ultimately to exile in Spain. His political party was declared illegal and any mention of his name or that of Evita was prohibited. Thus in the very month that saw Daimler-Benz decide to suspend racing, the government in Juan Fangio's homeland underwent the most profound turmoil and transformation.

As a post-Christmas present in 1955 to 172 companies and 586 individuals, Argentina's provisional government froze their assets until they could prove that they had legally acquired them during the Perón years. On the list of the individuals were industrialists, diplomats, sports stars, film and theatre actors and racing drivers – Fangio and González. They had 150 days to prove the legality of their rights to their property; thereafter their assets could be confiscated.

Fangio had little to fear. 'Politics, I think, are handled from behind a desk, not the wheel of a racing car,' he said. 'If the Perón government thought it hit a good idea to satisfy public enthusiasm for motor racing, what reason should I have to stop competing? But I chose never to do anything political, neither for nor against any government of my country, no matter which one. I hope no one will reproach me for that.' Fangio would be cleared by his government, but it would take agonising years, not mere months. In the meantime his assets were in cold storage; so, for the time being, had to be any thought of retirement.

When at the end of 1949 Evita Perón had suggested that the drivers should be given the Formula 2 Ferraris that had been bought for their European campaign, Benedicto Campos was kicking Juan under the table when he said that that was a bad idea, that the cars should be kept in Europe for the use of the next drivers coming from Argentina. Blessed beyond normal measure with both modesty and common sense, Fangio had been a symbol of the glories of Perón's Argentina, but he had never been seduced by them.

'The government has promised me a fair assessment of my situation,' Fangio said early in 1956. 'Actually I can say that I'm happy that a public determination will be made of the source of my property: it was earned with difficulty in many exhausting races. Naturally I will drive in Europe again this year, and my main goal is to win the world championship for a fourth time.'

This was Fangio's public posture, but privately he was less ecstatic about this threat to his affairs. 'Things started to go not so well in Argentina,' he said later, 'so I decided to postpone retirement for another year. I returned to Europe to race with Ferrari in 1956, but I wasn't very happy about it.' But why Ferrari and not his old love, Maserati?

The Orsis who owned the works of the trident had engaged a driver they thought nearly as good as Fangio, Stirling Moss, to join the thrusting Jean Behra in their 1956 team. Moss had tried but failed to find a British car he considered worthy and had vowed not to drive for the 'prancing horse' after, he felt, being two-timed by Ferrari at Bari in 1951.

For Fangio's part, he had not been best pleased by a kerfuffle over the winner's trophy between himself and the Maserati management, for whom he won the Caracas sports-car race with a 300S in November 1955, his first post-Mercedes race. That there might have been toing and froing over the trophy was not surprising. It was a solid gold cup weighing 5 kilograms – 11 pounds – which was later valued at some half a million dollars.

Equipment was a factor too, as Maserati's Ermanno Cozza pointed out: 'It's possible that Fangio chose Ferrari because at the time they had the Lancia cars, which were more innovative and promising, and he was always looking for the best car.' Added Maserati engineer Giulio Alfieri, 'He probably thought that Maserati wasn't up to his level in that period. There were also economic reasons.' *Ergo* – contacts with Ferrari.

'I saw him for the first time at the Modena Autodromo in 1949,' said Enzo Ferrari of Fangio. 'I watched him for a couple of laps and then I couldn't take my eyes off the car. His style was unique: he was probably the only driver to come out of a curve without grazing the bales of hay on the shoulder. "This Argentine is not kidding around," I told myself. "He comes out of the turns like a shot but he holds the middle of the track."'

'Later he came to talk to me at the Scuderia,' wrote Ferrari in his memoirs. 'He was accompanied by an official from the Argentine Automobile Club, and we all talked for quite a long time. Actually Fangio didn't say more than ten words. I couldn't figure him out. He evaded my glances, answered in monosyllables in a strange tinny voice and let others speak for him, an indefinable crooked little smile plastered across his face, making it impenetrable.'

Soon enough Enzo Ferrari was able to appreciate Fangio's abilities on the race track. But that didn't make the inscrutable bandy-legged man from the pampas any more appealing. 'As concerns Fangio as a man,' he said, 'our later conversations were no more successful than that first one. His gaze continued to evade mine, my questions continued to provoke enigmatic answers, which he gave in that strange little voice, and whoever happened to be with him would speak for him.' The oracular, mysterious role was usually Ferrari's. Here, for a change, was a man who did not seem cowed by the Merlin of Maranello.

When early in 1951 Alfa Romeo had seemed shy about a return to the tracks, Fangio's options had included the purchase of the new 4½-litre racer built by the Maserati brothers at OSCA or, indeed, buying a 4½-litre V12 from Ferrari and competing against the works team. Under no circumstances, however, would Ferrari sell Fangio a car, as he told Neubauer, because the Argentine would only grab the prize money that Ferrari needed in order to survive.

All this mattered not a whit at the end of 1955 to Fangio, who had decided to retire as a driver: 'That's why I hadn't given much importance to the meeting I had had with Enzo Ferrari. He had found out that I was at Pescara, where I was having a few days of relaxation at the end of the season. He phoned me and asked me to come and have a chat with him at Maranello: "Fangio, I know you cost a lot, but I need you." I remember those words of his very well.'

It could not have been easy for Ferrari to admit that he needed someone. He was a builder of great racing cars; thus the best drivers queued up for them. But just as circumstances had driven Alfa Romeo to need Fangio in 1950, so they conspired again in 1956. During 1955 Lancia had withdrawn from racing and turned over its complete stable of V8 single-seaters to Ferrari. Here were the only cars that had been able to rival the Mercedes on sheer speed; Ferrari had to be seen to do well with them in 1956, especially because he had also been heavily bankrolled to do so by Italian business interests including Fiat, which had underwritten an annual subsidy of £30,000. But the driver he loved, the consummate artist who had mastered the tricky Lancia, Alberto Ascari, had been killed in a test at Monza.

'I will take the drivers that no one else wants,' Ferrari boasted in 1956. 'I don't have the money to throw away on people. I will certainly have Castellotti and Musso, and above all the supreme champion Fangio.' But actually getting Fangio was another matter. 'Ferrari began a protracted and difficult negotiation to obtain his services,' wrote his biographer Brock Yates. 'There was trouble from the start. Ferrari was accustomed to dealing with drivers directly, without intermediaries. This was to his advantage. Most were naïve in the ways of business and could easily be bamboozled into driving for pittances. But Fangio was different. He had come from Mercedes-Benz, where drivers were paid handsomely, and was not about to accept Ferrari's menial sums – gift-wrapped in the potential 'glory' to be gained by a drive for the Scuderia.

'Fangio brought to the meetings a wily agent named Marcello Giambertone,' Yates continued, 'an Italian race promoter and general gadfly in the sport. Ferrari was furious at Fangio's effrontery in coming with an intermediary. Worse yet, Giambertone hammered out a lucrative deal for his client. It is said that Fangio received about 12 million lire a year for driving, plus a list of small perks that battered Ferrari's wallet. But whatever the deal, the relationship between the Commendatore and his star driver began on a sour note and never improved.' At the time that would have been worth $19,150, or £6,850.

According to Romolo Tavoni, then Ferrari's secretary, Giambertone did not seek a contract that resembled Fangio's with Mercedes. He may well have judged that to ask Ferrari for *all* the starting and prize money would be a complete non-starter. 'Usually Mr Ferrari split the prize money 50–50 with his drivers,' Tavoni told Chris Nixon. 'At Mercedes Fangio had been given 50 per cent *and* a big salary and he demanded the same at Ferrari.' This wasn't so, but it was a good enough negotiating position for Giambertone, who knew well that Ferrari's coffers as well as his stable had been replenished.

'Mr Ferrari liked Fangio the driver but not Fangio the man,' Tavoni continued, 'saying, "I provide the cars, you provide the driving skills, so I think 50–50 is correct." When Fangio insisted on a salary also, Ferrari felt that he was breaking with tradition.' Fangio was less interested in tradition than he was in stability and security; with a salary he knew where and when his next lira was arriving. Grudgingly, we may be sure, Enzo Ferrari agreed to Fangio's terms.

Ironically the first race of the 1956 season, at Buenos Aires in January, found Fangio driving the Lancia D50 that had been offered to him for 1954 by Gianni Lancia. Now, slightly modified, it wore a Ferrari badge. When asked how it compared to the Mercedes Juan Manuel answered, 'It's different.' It was also a second quicker in qualifying in Fangio's hands than his W196 had been the year before; he was a full two seconds clear of the field in pole position.

Helped by retirements, Fangio was able to win after taking over Luigi Musso's car when his own had fuel-pump trouble. This set a pattern for the season, although not one that was established by Ferrari team manager Eraldo Sculati, whom Fangio disliked and who in fact would only hold the post that season. Highly paid champion though he was, Fangio was not officially designated the team's number one driver. This was significant at a time when drivers could share cars and still earn points; the 'number one' man would have first choice in such situations. The drivers – Castellotti, Collins and Musso – took care of that, said Fangio: 'The young men told me, Juan, you are the leader, you are the world champion.'

At Buenos Aires Fangio's race fastest lap was an impressive three seconds quicker than the time he had clocked in the Mercedes (also the race's fastest lap) in 1955. Maserati protested a push-start Juan had received on the circuit, but their attempt to have him disqualified was rejected. 'Fangio himself is a splendid sportsman who plays fair and observes the rules,' remarked Mike Hawthorn, 'but it seems that when he gets out to Argentina he becomes the victim of over-enthusiastic helpers to whom all's fair as long as their national hero wins.'

With a full programme of sports-car races plus Formula 1 races both championship and non-championship, Ferrari worked his expensive driver hard in 1956. Only once during the year, in an Argentine sports-car race, did Ferrari fail to provide a car. Fangio won it in a Maserati 300S. In sports cars he always teamed with 26-year-old Eugenio Castellotti from Milan, nicknamed *'Il Bello'* for his good looks. They dominated in their 410 Sport Ferrari at Buenos Aires until its gearbox failed. In another Formula 1 race at Mendoza Fangio won single-handedly against a Moss-led Maserati phalanx after his team-mates retired.

Sports cars at Sebring were on the agenda next, and

for this 12-hour race Ferrari produced the ideal car, the four-cylinder 860 Monza. The early laps saw a vigorous battle between Mike Hawthorn's D-Type Jaguar, Stirling Moss in a DB3S Aston Martin and J. M. Fangio. Aston's Reg Parnell, deputed by team manager John Wyer to hold a more conservative pace, had a ringside seat.

'Reg told me later he had a brief but fascinating glimpse of this dice when the three cars lapped him,' wrote Wyer. 'Hawthorn came by first and Mike was totally "gone", concentrating 110 per cent and completely oblivious to anything around him. Then came Moss, considerably wound up but still with time to indicate to Reg that he'd like him to try and hold up Fangio for a couple of seconds. Finally – the Old Man himself, relaxed as ever and passing Reg with a courteous smile and a wave.'

The Grand Prix circus moved to Europe in April for non-championship contests at Siracusa and then, in May, at Silverstone. On the road circuit on the outskirts of the historic Sicilian city Fangio led from pole and set fastest lap en route to a dominant Lancia-Ferrari victory. Fangio's ill luck in Britain continued at Silverstone and he imposed it as well on Peter Collins at his home circuit by taking over Peter's car at one-third distance. Both Ferraris retired with clutch trouble and Moss won in a début drive in the new Vanwall.

At Monaco Fangio stamped his authority on an elite field of cars with a storming pole-position performance. The race was another story. 'Fangio was a crazy mixed-up racing driver that day,' said *Autosport*. His Ferrari was damaged in an early spin while chasing a leading Maserati-mounted Moss and damaged even more when its driver began using all the pavement and more in his furious chase. He brought the car in and at two-thirds distance was given that of Peter Collins, who was then in a strong second place. Collins, said *Autosport*, 'was so vexed that he went straight to his hotel and turned his back on the race passing its doors.'

Fangio couldn't catch Moss but his second-place Monaco finish saw him leading the championship. Nevertheless it had been a messy performance by his standards. 'Many people have said it was not Fangio in the car that day,' he told Nigel Roebuck, 'but they don't know what was going on in the car! For me it was the fastest way around that track in that car. It may not have been pretty to watch, but it *was* the quickest way.'

He knew a different style would be needed for the high-speed swerves of Spa in June. There in qualifying he was a staggering *five seconds* quicker than the next-fastest man, Stirling Moss. Although Stirling was first away at the start, he wrote that 'Fangio was all out to rehabilitate himself and win the world championship and passed me at the end of the Masta Straight.' The Argentine gained a commanding lead but suffered a transaxle failure at two-thirds distance, letting Peter Collins through to his first win in a championship Grand Prix.

The next championship GP a month later at Reims trailed by a week a battle royal between the 2-litre sports cars of Ferrari and Maserati at Monza. There, wrote Rodney Walkerley, 'the full temperament and brio of Italian opera and the backstage of international ballet had been reproduced in the pits, with mechanics in tears, drivers offering physical violence, team managers having near-hysterics, Fangio playing patience outside his pit in complete indifference to what was going on inside, and no one completely certain as to who was supposed to be driving with whom in what car.'

Hot from this stimulating atmosphere the teams arrived for the French GP at Reims with its daunting high-speed bend at Gueux. In qualifying Denis Jenkinson lent an ear to the sound of Fangio's Lancia-Ferrari: 'As he went past the pits at nearly 160mph everyone listened for him to lift his foot off the accelerator as he approached the long right-hand curve; the scream of the eight megaphones remained constant until it died away in the distance and everyone, drivers included, paid tribute to the world champion.' Eyebrows went sky-high afterward when Juan explained that he was having to hold the shift lever in fifth half-way around the curve because it was jumping out of gear!

Like Spa, Reims resulted in mechanical problems for Fangio while leading, this time a fuel line that sprung a leak. He had not necessarily expected Mercedes-style reliability at Ferrari, but this was beginning to niggle. Fangio thought that he had a solution. 'I had always had a mechanic exclusively on my car,' he said, 'but Ferrari had a different system. Half-way through the season I was able to arrange it, and then everything was much better.' Cassani was delegated to look after his cars.

An ex-mechanic himself, this was a requirement Juan Manuel understood. 'The driver must always have a relationship with his mechanic,' he felt. 'He must go to the garage and see what is going on. This is one thing which makes a relation between driver and mechanic turn into a friendship. It was this that I found hard to achieve in the Ferrari team. I had been their opposition for so many years and now I was their driver.'

It seemed to work. Reliability was in his favour at Silverstone, where Fangio scored his only victory on British soil when the race leader, Moss, retired. At the Nürburgring Fangio's Lancia-Ferrari had the legs of Moss's Maserati in both practice and the race, which Juan led from flag to flag. He was the first of several drivers who broke the lap record that Hermann Lang had set in 1939 in the 3-litre supercharged Mercedes-Benz. Of the five works Ferraris that started, his was the only one to finish.

Juan Fangio went to the last championship race of the season at Monza with a clear points lead and only a mathematical chance of losing the crown to Moss, Behra or Collins. Wrote Rodney Walkerley, 'We think Peter Collins is in the running somewhat to his own surprise and, like other drivers, will be glad if Fangio retains his honours and will be quite content to drive to Ferrari's team orders as usual. At least he has pulled himself out of the junior class where he is expected to hand over his car during a race.'

With the Italian Grand Prix being run on the road circuit and the bumpy high-speed banking combined, durability would be a factor at Monza, and so it proved. Ferrari had problems with both its Englebert tyres and the fragility of its steering arms. Fangio could finish the Mille Miglia with one wheel steering but not a Grand Prix at Monza, as he found just before half-distance. After 20 laps he brought his car to the pits. After long repairs Castellotti took it back into the fray.

There was Fangio, standing carless in the pit lane. A stony-faced Musso, hoping to do well on his home ground, ignored him during a tyre change. De Portago had retired his Ferrari early. Juan's only hope of taking the championship well out of the reach of the leading Moss was Peter Collins, circulating in third place. Collins, for his part, would have to win *and* set fastest lap to out-point Fangio.

Collins knew what he would do. His bitter emotions over Monaco had been forgotten. Walkerley's assessment had been spot-on. Stopping for tyres on lap 34 Collins made it clear that he expected Fangio to take over his car. Out of the junior class or not, the 25-year-old from Kidderminster felt it was too soon for him to be wresting the championship crown from Fangio. 'I was astonished when he handed over his car,' said Juan, 'but I did not stop to argue. I do not know whether in his place I would have done the same. Collins was the gentleman driver.'

In Collins's Ferrari Juan Fangio finished second in the Italian Grand Prix, only six seconds behind a Moss who was lucky to win after an emergency fuel top-up and the retirement of Musso, who led until three laps from the finish. Thanks to the coup that led to the exile of Juan Perón, championship pretenders Moss, Collins, Musso and Castellotti would have to wait their turn. Juan Fangio topped the world championship standings for the fourth time in all and the third time running.

It had been a hard battle for Fangio, as demanding as his 1951 season. He began the year on equal terms with his young rivals, who were widely expected to see him off. He ended the year as the towering artist of his craft who seemed still to have reserves of speed and skill. As for Enzo Ferrari, he felt he got what he paid for. It had been a difficult year for him, with the death of his son Alfredo 'Dino' on 30 June, the Saturday before the French Grand Prix. He was resigned about the future. In 1957, he said, 'we won't have the world champion. We won't have him because we don't have enough money.'

Although familiar, this photo is well worth seeing again for its portrayal of the artistry and accuracy with which Juan Fangio attacks the fast curves of Britain's Silverstone circuit. He retires in this May race in the Ferrari-modified Lancia but is victorious later in the season in the British Grand Prix.

A I L Y
1

In the V8-powered Lancia-Ferrari Fangio is racing toward retirement at Silverstone in May 1956 (above) and toward a decisive victory in the German Grand Prix at the Nürburgring in August (opposite top). In the season's final GP at Monza (bottom) he leads Peter Collins, who generously hands over his Ferrari when Fangio's breaks so that the Argentine can confirm his fourth world drivers' championship.

By the end of the 1956 season at Monza Enzo Ferrari (above right) can be happy with the return on his expensive investment in Juan Fangio. Although not officially so designated, Fangio is accepted as the team's leader by young colleagues like (below right, left to right) Peter Collins, Fon de Portago and Castellotti. Fangio appreciates the support and encouragement he receives from his Ferrari team-mates, especially from likeable young Briton Peter Collins (left top and bottom).

Two starts at Silverstone in 1956 (5 May above and 14 July below) have the same result: Mike Hawthorn rockets away in the BRM to an early retirement. Fangio (1) retires in the first instance and is victorious in the second, his only win on British soil. His August success in the German G.P. comes after he argues for a mechanic to be in specific charge of his car following a fuel-line split at Reims in July (overleaf) that drops him from the lead to a fourth-place finish.

10

10

Continental
Continental
CONTINENTAL
CONTINENTAL

Although he detests the Le Mans-type starts at which Stirling Moss (5) excels, Fangio is nevertheless willing to sign up to drive the first stint, as he does at the Nürburgring for the 1956 1000-kilometre race. With Castellotti he brings his Ferrari (1) home in second place.

600

Juan Fangio finishes a wet and weary fourth in the 1956 Mille Miglia in his 290MM Ferrari (600). Holes cut to drain water from the cockpit instead pour it into the car: 'Towards the finish my hands were frozen stiff. I could neither unclench my fingers nor grasp the wheel and gear shift properly. I was numb right through and shivering. I really abused my body that day. It was my hardest race.' A warmer and happier contest is Sebring in March (17), where he and Castellotti take their 860 Monza Ferrari through to victory in the 12-hour race.

S-BENZ
's in sich!
ER Reifen
SCH
BOSCH
ifen

CHAPTER 7

At the trident's peak

When Juan Fangio first began doing business with Maserati in 1948 the small Modena company was in a peculiar state. Founded in 1926 by the four Maserati brothers, the company had accepted a majority shareholder in 1937: the Orsi family. Commendatore Adolfo Orsi already controlled the Modena steel mill, factories making agricultural equipment and transport interests, including the local trolleybus concession. He had acquired Maserati less for its fine racing cars than for its sideline as a spark-plug producer.

In May 1947, at the end of the ten years that they had agreed to remain after the takeover, the three surviving brothers left Maserati and returned to their homes in Modena. Fine craftsmen remained; they still produced Maseratis for customers like the Argentine Automobile Club. Preoccupied as he was with his own post-war business problems, which now included machine tools and electric trucks, Adolfo Orsi paid relatively little attention to Maserati. He and Fangio had met in 1948, however, and had hit it off.

As he completes lap three of the 22-lap 1957 German Grand Prix Juan Fangio is building up the early advantage over the Ferraris of Hawthorn and Collins that will allow him to make a pit stop for fuel and fresh tyres. This sets the stage for one of the most exciting finishes in the history of the sport.

At the urging of Adolfo's son Omer, the car company's managing director, Maserati re-established a racing arm in time to build the 2-litre Grand Prix cars that hospitalised Juan Fangio in 1952 and took him to a spectacular victory at Monza at the end of 1953. Having ended the season on this high note with Fangio, Adolfo and Omer Orsi were keen to keep him on their strength for 1954. In this campaign they had some valuable assets.

One such asset was Guerrino Bertocchi, a reservoir of Maserati experience who functioned as both chief racing mechanic and test driver. Although not in the Rudy Uhlenhaut class, he could test a fast car's mettle. Importantly, he had Fangio's confidence. Another asset through 1953 was Gioachino Colombo, who had significantly improved that season's Maserati. Fangio had much appreciated the way Colombo had shaped up the Alfa Romeo attack in 1951. Colombo, however, was lured away in October by Pierre Marco, who engaged him to design a completely new Bugatti Formula 1 car.

The intense yet practical Vittorio Bellentani took over Maserati engineering.

The Orsis had another enticing asset, the glistening machine that Colombo had left behind: a new Formula 1 car originally called the 250/F1 and later simply 250F. The Orsis did all they could to exploit their Monza victory to promote the sales of their new racer. At the works they showed potential customers a non-running mock-up of the car with its new 2½-litre twin-cam six-cylinder engine, powerful brakes, ingenious transaxle and de Dion rear suspension. Inert though it was, with its curvaceous lines and swathes of louvres it was gorgeous.

After the Italian Grand Prix one of the 2-litre team cars was made available for a few laps of Monza by some of the drivers who might like to buy a 250F, among them Fangio's friend Johnny Claes, American John Fitch, Roy Salvadori, Louis Rosier and Harry Schell. This 1953 car could be, and was, updated for 1954 racing by installing the new 250F engine. Built up for early testing, one such car was ready before Fangio returned to Argentina. It's likely that on a cool October day he had a chance to try it at the Modena Autodromo. Thus Juan had a lot to think about when he returned to Argentina and his occasional chats with Baron von Korff.

By November Fangio had learned the generous terms of the contract Daimler-Benz was prepared to offer. Having reasonable faith in the company's ability to put a good car under him, he considered himself committed to the Stuttgart firm. But Mercedes-Benz would not have its new car ready until mid-year while the Argentine *Temporada* races – command performances for the nation's premier driver – would begin in mid-January. What would Fangio drive against the Ferrari and Gordini works teams? Ferrari was challenging him by fielding his arch-rivals González, Farina and Hawthorn.

Maserati's 250F was ready – just barely. Bertocchi had turned its baptismal laps at the Autodromo in December. Negotiating cables flew between the Orsis and the Argentine Auto Club to bring two of the cars to Buenos Aires for Fangio and 'Pinocho' Marimon, who had impressed with his strong performance at Monza. Agreement was reached that Maserati's cars would come as works entries but with a heavy financial commitment from the Auto Club. Maserati just managed its end of the deal. Its mechanics worked through Christmas to get two 250Fs ready for the last possible boat to Argentina, sailing on 26 December.

Although two new 250Fs went to Argentina only one could be raced, such was the engine attrition owing to oiling problems. In desperation Bertocchi bought up supplies of olive oil and mixed it with the engine oil to try to suppress the frothing that was ruining engine bearings. Cooling was a problem too in the heat of the Argentine summer; a slot was cut in the nose to admit more air. In the Grand Prix this was alleviated by showers that helped Fangio take the lead after a stop for rain-treaded tyres.

Thinking wishfully that the Argentine would be disqualified for too many mechanics working on his car at that stop, the Ferrari team manager did not press his drivers to attack. Fangio came home more than a minute ahead of Farina as the winner of the first Grand Prix of the new Formula 1. He also gave the new Maserati 250F a victory in its first race, an uncommon distinction in the world of racing cars.

This was a rare bright spot in the increasingly cloudy regime of Juan Perón, for whom the chance to sit in Fangio's car after the race was a cheering photo opportunity. It was precious publicity too for the Orsis, whose companies had valuable trading relations with Argentina. There was something in it for Fangio as well: when from time to time he sold Maseratis into South America he would earn a commission of 5 or 6 per cent.

For Fangio's part he was happy still to be driving a Maserati: 'I was very pleased to be racing for Count Orsi and for his son Omer, two great gentlemen whose correctness and courtesy could only be compared with the invariably proper attitude of the Mercedes and Alfa Romeo directors, as I remembered them.' This was reciprocated on the Maserati side, said engineer Giulio Alfieri: 'It was a relationship of great respect and fidelity, based on his personal relations with Orsi and Guerrino Bertocchi.'

Although Juan had shrewdly nursed his Maser to a win at Buenos Aires he had to retire a fortnight later in a non-championship Argentine race. In April Fangio was expected at Siracusa and in June at Rome, both non-championship races, but he failed to appear, so apart from his March stint at Sebring for Lancia he would not race until the Belgian Grand Prix at Spa on 20 June – again in a 250F.

That didn't mean that Fangio wasn't driving Maseratis. As the new 250Fs were being completed in the spring he would usually test each car at the Autodromo. This was an important insurance policy for the Orsis, whose customers could hardly complain that their cars weren't up to scratch if Fangio had already driven them, and quickly. Raymond Mays personally thanked Juan Manuel for test-driving the 250F bought by the BRM team as a practice and race car before their own new racer was ready. Also, said Alfieri, 'When he was in Modena he used to borrow a Maserati, just for fun.'

Both the man and the car were ready for Spa. Given a new higher rev limit after improvements to the engine, Fangio began duelling for pole with the Ferrari of González. He triumphed with a staggering 120.5mph lap on this daunting road course that equalled the qualifying record he had set there in 1951 with the far more powerful Alfetta. Anthony Pritchard wrote that 'back at the pits the 250F was leaking oil from just about every joint, the brakes were red hot and the car shimmered in a haze of heat.'

In the race, which was filmed for *The Racers* on the big screen, Fangio was slow away but was soon battling for the lead with his old rival, Ferrari-mounted Nino Farina. After the latter's retirement Fangio was under less pressure, which was just as well as the Maserati was visibly sagging, having broken bits of its suspension, and at the end was steaming from a holed radiator. Juan was justly gaining a reputation as a driver who was not only fast but also had an uncanny knack for nursing an injured car to a respectable finish – even, as on this occasion, to victory.

A week later at Monza Fangio was paired with Marimon at the wheel of the pretty A6GCS/2000 Maserati sports car. They were running second in the six-hour race when mechanical trouble knocked them out of contention. Apart from two sports-car races in the 1955–56 winter season, which he would win in the 300S, Juan Fangio would not race a Maserati again until 1957. His Mercedes-Benz and Ferrari years would follow.

Fangio's decision to return to Maserati in 1957 had not been difficult to take. One season with Enzo Ferrari had been enough for both men. Besides, as Maserati's Cozza said, 'Those cars were not as good as he expected.'

Britain's up-and-coming Vanwall team had approached Juan in 1956, but he had seen the car as still too immature. A contact was made again about the 1957 season, but, wrote Jenkinson and Posthumus, 'the Argentinian made it known that he would not consider joining the Vanwall team as he did not want to upset Stirling Moss, accepting that Stirling's rightful place was at the head of the British team.' In any case, Fangio had added in artful misdirection, he was thinking of retiring. Vanwall's Tony Vandervell did not give up easily; he brought a spare Vanwall to Rouen in mid-season in the hopes that Fangio would try it, but the offer was politely declined.

Visiting the Maserati works at the end of his 1956 season, Juan Fangio found that the Orsis and their new chief engineer, Giulio Alfieri, had not been idle. An impressive new sports-racing car, the V8 450S, had already been seen in experimental form. A formidable new V12 engine was being built to power the 250F. Lessons learned with the special offset cars built for the Italian Grand Prix were being incorporated in a completely new 250F for 1957 that would only be raced by the factory; just three were being made. And Maserati was brewing up another speed secret: a judicious addition of oxygen-bearing nitromethane to the fuel blend, which brought an impressive power increase.

Fangio and Adolfo Orsi shook hands on a co-operation for 1957, a traditional 50–50 sharing of starting and prize money. Their relationship was one of friendship and mutual respect, 'a very frank relationship,' said Giulio Alfieri, 'without being ashamed of saying no. Sometimes he would come back a year later and race on the same car he had refused' – as he was doing now. 'Maserati never had a formal agreement with Fangio, partly because of his very good relationship with Commendatore Orsi. They thought that their word was good enough. Maserati was a small firm and relations with its racers were on a personal basis. Only big companies had legal agreements with their drivers. With a big shot like Fangio a formal agreement wasn't necessary.'

'They had changed their 250F model considerably since I first drove them in 1954,' Fangio said of Maserati. 'The car was lighter, had a bit more power and had ended up very well balanced. You could do what you liked in that sort of car. It was nicely poised, responsive, fast and suited my driving style.'

British driver Roy Salvadori had an on-track view of just how well the 250F suited Fangio: 'My most vivid and unforgettable memory of a car being driven on, or even past, the limit was a 250F Maserati being thrown round the Nürburgring and Rouen circuits by Juan Fangio, both of which races he won. While undoubtedly Fangio was the fastest driver of the era, and probably of all time, he needed a forgiving car to make these feats possible, and that is exactly what the 250F was.' Theirs was a marriage that made 1957 memorable for both.

There were sports-car races to run as well. Moss and Fangio, rivals on the Grand Prix circuits, were team-mates for Maserati. Fangio eschewed the Mille Miglia that year and was on hand at Le Mans as a reserve driver to keep the opposition on its toes. Although he didn't race, he set a new absolute record for the track, an average of 126.5mph, during practice in the powerful 450S roadster. He was destined to win only one race in this car, the 12 Hours of Sebring when paired with Jean Behra.

In fact Fangio might not have raced for Maserati at Sebring. His old Chevrolet loyalties had been reawakened by Corvette engineer Zora Arkus-Duntov, who was secretly building a dramatic new sports-racing car, the Corvette SS. It was to make its debut at Sebring and Juan Fangio had agreed to drive it – subject, of course, to his approval of the car. Because the SS was so late – it wasn't even raceworthy at the start – he never had a chance to test it and was released to Maserati.

But Fangio did drive a 'muletta' version of the SS in Sebring's Friday practice. Driver Bill Pollack was there: 'Fangio took to it like he had been in the car all of his life and came within two one-hundredths of his own track record. Needless to say, there were a lot of raised eyebrows in the Corvette pits. I was in the pits when Fangio got out of the car. He turned to the astonished Chevy executives and said something like "Nice car", and walked away.'

Driving a 2-litre Maserati, Pollack was battling in the race with Richie Ginther in a Ferrari of similar size. 'The hairpin was always a close fight between Richie and me,' Pollack said. 'Each time I would go as deep as possible before getting on the brakes. This was further complicated by a washboard surface just before the turn. If you blew the turn you were in a very bad spot that would require a tow car and extensive repairs. Just as I was entering this difficult part of the course, Fangio in the big 4½-litre came by both of us, off-line for the corner, turned to me and gave me the high sign. Richie and I were on the verge of losing it and this man could do the impossible in a larger car.

'I am sure that everyone who races thinks that he or she is pretty fast,' Bill Pollack reflected, 'and, given a comparable car, would be as fast as anyone on the track. Meeting Fangio was a humbling experience. He wasn't just faster than everyone else. He was in another league! Watching him with the tired Corvette and the big Maserati made me feel like I was a student in "Racing 101". Fortunately, I got over it. But Fangio was awfully good.'

But was he good enough to defend his championship status against the young lions who were growling at his heels? 'My opponents that year were all young fellows, Moss, Collins and Hawthorn,' he reflected. 'They called me the "Old Man" and I suppose I was. They could have been my sons, but they didn't have the experience in racing that I had, and experience is very important.' He drew on all his experience, and then some, in 1957.

A slight chink in his armour was revealed in the first championship Grand Prix of 1957 in January: Moss outqualified him for the pole at Buenos Aires, of all places, in identical Maseratis and Jean Behra was only 0.3 of a second slower in the third new car. 'The start was chaotic,' said Moss, 'as it often is, and before the parade the crowd invaded the circuit intent on mobbing their idol, Fangio.' They mobbed him afterward as well, celebrating a lucky victory over Jean Behra helped by a quicker stop for fuel. Fangio won again in a non-championship two-heat race a fortnight later. His season was off to a good start.

Racing resumed in Europe at Monaco in May. Fangio stamped his authority on the proceedings with a pole-winning practice time in his usual 250F after a valiant struggle with the V12 on a most unsuitable circuit for its peaky power curve. On the fourth lap, following Moss and Collins, Juan Manuel again demonstrated his phenomenal powers of anticipation and response. The brakes on Stirling's Vanwall played up and he went straight on at the chicane, followed by Collins.

'At that moment I arrived on the scene,' said Fangio. 'I saw posts, torn up by the two cars, rolling in a haphazard way towards the centre of the track. I managed to brake just enough to arrive in the middle of that confusion at no more than walking pace. My right wheels went over a post, jolting the Maserati but nothing more, and I went straight off, taking advantage of the clear road. Behind me the posts continued rolling, almost entirely barring the road.' They caught Hawthorn as well.

'That Fangio managed to get through was typical of his amazing perception,' thought Moss, 'because this was not the only occasion when his ability to size up a situation saved him from disaster.' Indeed, he had done so at the same circuit seven years earlier. 'I have always looked upon Fangio as the greatest driver who ever lived and still do,' Moss continued. 'To my mind he was in his prime in 1955 and 1956 and I had the feeling in 1957 that he was having to try quite hard to be fastest where before it had just come naturally and easily.'

He kept trying hard at Monaco: 'All the young English boys except Brooks were out and I was left alone in the lead. Brooks put tremendous pressure on me, but I just drove harder to break his heart. Finally he relaxed and settled for second. And I relaxed and settled for first.' The doggedness of Tony Brooks in pursuit made an impression on Fangio, Alf Francis recalled: 'Bertocchi has more opportunities than most people of talking to Fangio, and after Monaco the great Argentine driver told him that Brooks would be the next world champion.' With Ferrari, in 1959, he came very close.

Neither Moss nor Brooks was fit enough to drive for Vanwall in the French GP at Rouen-les-Essarts, which was a pity because both would have revelled as Fangio did in the smooth, sinuous curves of this picture-book circuit. On his way to an unchallenged victory from pole Juan Manuel put on the demonstration of controlled power-sliding that had so impressed Roy Salvadori, watching from the seat of his Vanwall. A week later in a non-championship race at Reims Fangio was less happy, never leading and being classified eighth after coming off the road at the Thillois corner.

In the following weekend's British Grand Prix on the flat and unrewarding Aintree track Fangio was never in the picture. Feeling off-colour, he qualified fourth fastest and was running seventh when his engine let go. This had been Behra's turn to star for Maserati, but he retired to hand victory to a Vanwall successively crewed by Brooks and Moss – the first championship event victory for the British marque.

Fangio maintained a lead in the world championship but he hoped to put it on ice at the next race on the Nürburgring. He accepted the strategy proposed by Ugolini and Bertocchi, which was to run as light as possible and refuel, with fresh tyres, at the mid-race point. This would be easier on the car on the bumpy, hilly 'Ring. Ferrari, in contrast, elected to run non-stop.

In practice Fangio set the pace by carving *26 seconds* off his record pole time of the year before. He had three seconds in hand over his closest rival, Mike Hawthorn. And the night before the race he was relaxing with Beba and friends in the Sporthotel's restaurant past 11 o'clock. 'No one who saw him,' wrote Uli Wieselmann, 'could have the impression that he was contemplating the demanding race of the following day with particular tension or even excitement.'

In the race he let the Ferraris of Hawthorn and Collins lead at first. Fangio was always careful to bed in his Pirelli tyres before demanding more of them. Then he passed the Ferraris and set about building up the 30-second margin Bertocchi had told him he'd need for his pit stop. His third lap was a new record, and so were his fifth, sixth, eighth and tenth. He broke records, wrote Rodney Walkerley, 'with a machine-like regularity that left us gasping, but his car was never straight, nose pointing off the road, wheels clipping the verges in the most breath-taking exhibition of driving since Nuvolari.'

Fangio's stop was on the 12th of 22 laps, when he had a 28-second lead. He hopped out of the car and selected a new pair of goggles while the mechanics made a total muddle of the refuelling and rear-tyre change, taking four seconds short of a minute instead of the promised half of that. Back in the race, his first laps were deceptively calm. Again, he was settling in his new tyres. But on the long 'Ring with pit signals only every 9½ minutes for the leaders, he was also misleading the Ferrari pit management. Collins and Hawthorn, blithely confident, were signalling each other that the latter should win.

Then the new lap records started coming for Fangio: the 17th, 18th and 19th. 'I started using third where I'd been using second and fourth where I'd been using third,' he said. Walkerley: 'Lap 20 and uproar in the grandstands, hysteria in the Ferrari pit; they gesticulated and tore the air, they fell on their knees to their drivers, and in the Maserati box Ugolini smiled at his watch. Fangio was on their tail – three seconds behind' the two British chums. On the next lap he passed them, first Collins then Hawthorn, who held on grimly to finish 3.6 seconds behind. Juan Fangio, renowned for his poker face in the cockpit, flew by the chequered flag with a huge grin.

'What a celebration there was! I was carried here, there and everywhere on people's shoulders,' he told Robert Carozzo. 'When I managed to get to the podium, Hawthorn and Collins were ecstatic, as if they had been the winner. They never stopped congratulating me and shaking me by the hand, even though my car had thrown up a stone and broken one of the lenses of Peter's goggles. Both truly appreciated me and their congratulations were sincere.

'Without any doubt, the Nürburgring was my favourite circuit,' added Fangio. 'I loved it, all of it, and I think that day I conquered it. On another day it might have conquered me, who knows? But I believe that day I took myself and my car to the limit, and perhaps a little bit more. That day I made such demands on myself that I couldn't sleep for two days afterwards. I was in such a state that whenever I shut my eyes it was as if I were in the race again, making those leaps in the dark on those curves where I had never before had the courage to push things so far.'

The rest of the season was anticlimactic. Finishing second behind Moss's powerful Vanwall in the last two championship races at Pescara and Monza was nothing to be ashamed of; their points gave Juan Fangio an awesome final margin over Stirling Moss.

His tip for the future, Tony Brooks, was given a driving lesson at Monza's daunting Curva Grande. 'We'd approach at about 175, I suppose, dab the brakes and go through at about 160,' he told Nigel Roebuck. 'I thought I was taking this corner pretty quickly, and in the early stages I was dicing with Fangio for the lead. First time through, touch the brakes, turn in – wham! Fangio goes by on the inside, oversteering it on the throttle! Later in the lap I got past again, then next time into the corner – wham! Exactly the same thing again. I don't know, maybe he wasn't braking at all.' The lesson to Brooks was the same as to Johnny Claes at Spa: 'Less brakes, and more accelerator.'

'He became world champion on Alfa Romeo, Mercedes-Benz, Ferrari and Maserati,' wrote Uli Wieselmann after the race at the 'Ring, 'and there's no doubt at all that he would have won the German Grand Prix driving the Ferrari of his rivals. From Fangio's drive one thing was clear: compared to his capabilities the entire world elite is blown into the second rank. His mastery is unique and unattainable, and I don't think that I'm speaking too excessively if I say that Fangio is the greatest racing driver of all time.' One hundred thousand ecstatic people around the Nürburgring that day, shouting themselves hoarse and throwing everything they owned into the air, would have agreed.

Feeling much at home with Maserati in Argentina, Juan Fangio – unusually dressed in a driving suit – shows off the new Maserati 250F to friends and fans after winning the 1954 Argentine Grand Prix. He drives it to victory in the first two championship races that year.

2

Fangio and Maserati pair well in 1954. He compares notes with chief engineer Giulio Alfieri (above left) and dines with proprietor Adolfo Orsi (above right). Early in 1954 Fangio shakes down a customer's 250F under the watchful eye of Bertocchi (below right) at the Modena Autodromo and compares notes there with Nino Farina in the presence of Maserati engineer Alberto Massimino (below left).

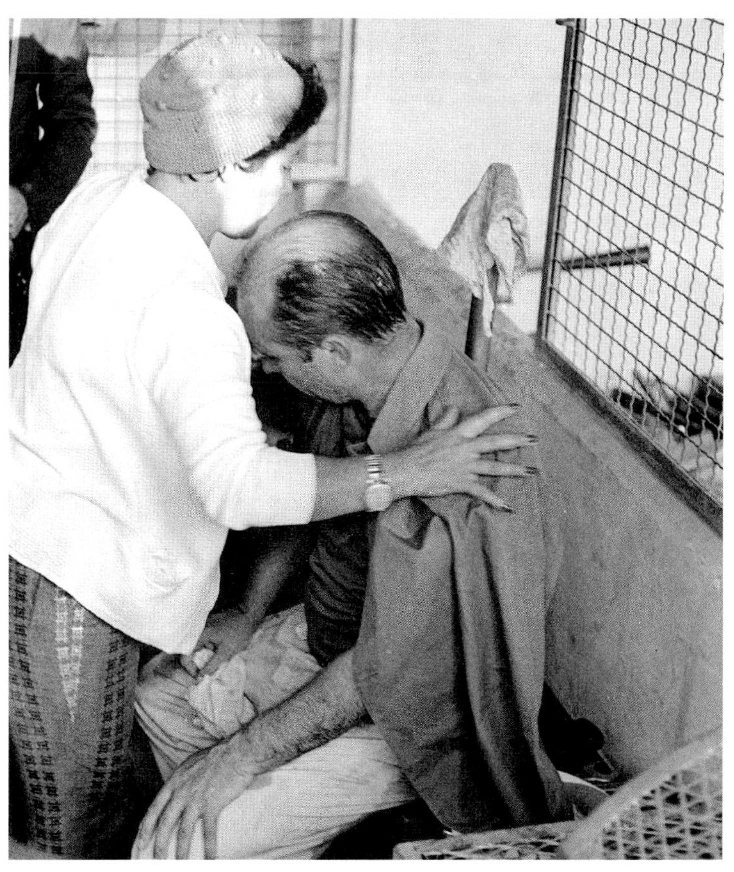

Turning 46 during the 1957 season, Fangio shows the strain of keeping up with his younger rivals. He is joined by team manager Nello Ugolini after his Monte Carlo victory (below right) and comforted by Beba after yielding to Stirling Moss in the Italian Grand Prix (above left).

Fangio makes a successful start to his 1954 season by winning at Buenos Aires in the 250F Maserati (above and preceding pages) and in the Belgian Grand Prix at Spa (opposite top). The great 250F is recognisably the same albeit completely different when Fangio returns to the team for the 1957 Argentine Grand Prix (below), which he wins. He is driving a car with the same serial number (2529) when he scores his memorable victory in the German Grand Prix, seen there in the Carousel (opposite bottom).

At Maserati in 1957 one of Fangio's team-mates is thrusting Frenchman Jean Behra. They compare notes among the fuel tins during practice for the Sebring 12 Hours, with Bernard Cahier snapping in the background. Their interchanges have an air of complicity at the Nürburgring (above) and Sebring (below).

At Sebring in 1957 Fangio tries the six-cylinder 300S during practice (above), a type with which he enjoys several successes, but elects instead to race the big 4.5-litre V8 450S with Jean Behra (below). They score a victory on the Florida airport-cum-road circuit.

Chased by the Ferrari of Peter Collins and the Maserati of Harry Schell, Fangio (32) and Moss (18) in the Vanwall make haste at the start of the 1957 Pescara Grand Prix. Fangio places second behind Moss. Bernard Cahier captures the style of both car and driver at Pescara (below).

Fangio delights his fans with a display of drifting driving at Rouen to win the French Grand Prix in July (above). By the penultimate 1957 championship Grand Prix at Monza (below and overleaf) Fangio has already secured his fifth world title.

Before the start he shares the grid with the V12 Maserati of Behra (6) and the Vanwalls of Moss (18) and Tony Brooks (22). Brooks's determined drives during the season prompt Fangio to tip him as a future champion.

2
2

Clockwise from the top the start unfolds for the dramatic 1957 Grand Prix of Germany at the Nürburgring. Hawthorn (8) and Collins (7) believe they control the race with their Ferraris until Fangio rudely overtakes them in the final laps. The defeated Hawthorn, helmetless below, joins enthusiastically in the celebrations of the great and determined drive that takes the 1957 drivers' world championship out of reach of Fangio's rivals.

CHAPTER 8

Hurricane's eye

Indianapolis had never been off Juan Fangio's agenda. Indy was where Argentina's pre-war motor-racing heroes, like Raul Riganti, had buffed their reputations abroad. Fangio's fact-finding team made the Indiana oval and its 500-mile race the first stop in their 1948 tour, before travelling on to Europe. Its spectacle and speed made a profound impression. Juan vowed to return to race there one day.

His first opportunity to race at Indianapolis was pencilled in his 1951 agenda. After their *Temporada* outing the Mercedes-Benz team were planning to compete at Indy, where the racing formula was still the same as in Europe before the war. Also, the 500-mile race counted for world championship points as a sop to the 'world' part of that designation; picking up points there would be a distinct bonus. Lacking the time needed to prepare his cars after their delayed return from Argentina, Neubauer had to scrub that plan.

Although naturally shy at first, Fangio is soon befriended by European drivers, among them Belgian Johnny Claes. At Reims in 1954 Juan literally shakes hands with photographer Rudy Mailander.

During their February 1954 discussions over Fangio's first Daimler-Benz contract, Baron von Korff told Alfred Neubauer that 'Fangio would like to drive at Indianapolis, to be sure on some sort of American car, not only because this race is highly regarded here but also because this would be looked on positively and supported by Mr Antonio (in connection with the new Argentine-American friendship!).' Juan Antonio of Mercedes-Benz Argentina would personally lead the financing of an Indy campaign for Juan Manuel.

Although Fangio's schedule would easily have accommodated it, it didn't happen that year. After Sebring in 1954, however, he did fly to Indy to take a few laps of the track in a sports car at the suggestion of its manager, former racer Wilbur Shaw. Contacts made at Sebring in 1956 led to an invitation to race at Indy for the successful John Zink team that year, but his Ferrari commitments ruled that out.

Competing at Indy wasn't all that unusual for some of Fangio's closest rivals. Alberto Ascari had performed creditably there in a Ferrari in 1952, only to retire, while Nino Farina had tried but failed to qualify for the race in 1956 and 1957. But when in 1957 the Indy stars and cars came to Monza to compete against their European counterparts on the banked track, the latter demurred. When Fangio joined the Grand Prix drivers who boycotted the first 'Race of Two Worlds' it generated mutterings among the Americans that he was not a 'real' world champion.

Semi-retired from Grand Prix racing in 1958, Fangio at last had time to mount an Indy attack. In a bizarre prelude he was invited by the DA Lubricant team to compete in the Trenton, New Jersey, 100-mile race that March. Although he declined, he did drive the DA Special sprint car for several dozen laps of the Trenton Fairgrounds oval. Meanwhile for the Indy 500 his manager Marcello Giambertone negotiated an agreement with Dayton, Ohio, industrialist George Walther Jnr to try his Offy-powered Dayton Steel Foundry Special, actually a Kurtis 500G built in 1957. The link with Walther had been a former Alfa Romeo engineer who was working at Dayton.

Juan arrived at the Speedway on 1 May and cruised through the physical and the mandatory rookie acclimatisation. When in the second week he started driving for speed, however, the Walther car suffered sundry technical problems that cut into his track time – unhelpful when trying to learn a new discipline. He was dismayed to find that his mechanics 'couldn't get a four-cylinder engine in trim, which is the simplest thing in the world.'

Indy veterans were amazed by the line Fangio took in negotiating the four-cornered oval. He charged deeper into the turns and hit the apexes earlier, exploiting his car-control skill on a track that rewards smoothness along its traditional 'groove'. 'I never saw anyone go faster out of the groove,' said 1958 winner Jimmy Bryan. 'From what I'd seen of him at Indianapolis he had to be a hell of a race driver just to maintain control of his Offy roadster,' said ace mechanic Clint Brawner, 'the silly way he was driving it in the corners. Fangio seemed to have his own idea of how to negotiate the corners. But the line he was taking was not the right one.'

Right line or not, good car or not, the fastest he could lap was 142.8mph when the quick speeds were around 145 – which he had set as his target. That was in fact 2.4mph faster than the same car had qualified in 1957 when it was brand new. Though doubtful about Walther's racer, Fangio wasn't familiar with the Indy ethos that drivers were free to hop from car to car to find one to qualify. A hint of what might have been, however, came when he tried Lew Welch's supercharged V8 Novi, a car of such awesome power that it scared most drivers. In only three laps Juan had it up to 135mph with much more to come.

Uncomfortable with his speed, car and team, and with insufficient time remaining to make a change, facing possible fuel wrangles over his personal contract with BP and disenchanted by some of the more sophomoric antics of the mid-western Americans, Juan Fangio had left Indianapolis by mid-May. He left with praise, however, for the way he had been treated and the unstinting guidance and hospitality he had received. He paid tribute to 'the wonderful atmosphere of clean, healthy sportsmanship prevailing there – this being the main reason why I consider my otherwise disheartening Indianapolis venture one of the most enjoyable experiences of my life.'

Juan Fangio was never shy about crediting the role that luck had played in his racing career. 'There is a formula for success,' he said, 'and it is not difficult to analyse. It is made up of 50 per cent car, 25 per cent driver and 25 per cent luck. All my life I have been lucky.' He may well have been lucky in failing to qualify for Indy that year.

Mike Magill qualified the Dayton Kurtis-Offy at 142.3mph on the second weekend, which meant he was well back in the field at the start. If Fangio had qualified at a similar speed on the first weekend he would have been much farther forward. In fact he might well have been in the midst of the 15-car accident that was triggered at the front of the field on the first lap by a spinning Ed Elisian. Unfamiliar with Speedway mores, Fangio could easily have been caught up in the resulting mayhem that caused many injuries and one fatality.

If Indy had been disheartening for him, the 1958 Race of Two Worlds at Monza was positively infuriating for Fangio – or would have been for someone of a less equable disposition. This was the Europeans' chance to avenge the humiliation they had suffered from their

1957 non-appearance. American shipper Al Dean, who had offered Fangio a car for Indianapolis, now did the same for Monza – the very car in which Jimmy Bryan had won the 1957 edition, specially beefed-up for Monza's bumpy bankings by Clint Brawner.

'Fangio was a baggy, balding man,' Brawner recalled for Joe Scalzo, who 'really wanted to win at Monza to prove himself. He promised me a $2,000 bonus if the car won. Because Fangio's legs were shorter than Bryan's, he had a hard time reaching the pedals at first. Also Fangio refused to fasten his seat belts, insisting he preferred to be thrown clear in the event of an accident. He *sat* on his belts.'

That Juan Fangio could still have new experiences this late in his racing career was testified to by Clint Brawner, who was 'worried that all the power of an Offy might unnerve him' – unnerve the man who had taken to the 500-horsepower BRM like a duck to water. Lest Fangio find the experience of herding an Offy too daunting, Brawner gave him only two-thirds throttle at first!

'Even without full power,' said the amazed mechanic, 'Fangio immediately turned a lap of better than 170. Once I gave him full throttle, Fangio got the roadster up to 175. I tell you, the man was a race driver.' 'The man' qualified equal third fastest in a 19-car field at an average for three laps of 171.4mph. 'He's no slob,' said one admiring American.

Race day, however, was a mega-fiasco. In the morning when Brawner was changing plugs he discovered cracks in the Offy's front and rear pistons. He laboured through both of the race's first two heats to replace them and finally had Fangio ready to attack the third and last heat – only to have an improperly installed fuel pump fall off. 'I felt rotten about it,' said Brawner. 'Without changing those pistons, Fangio might have been able to lead the race. He was capable of leading it. He might have blown up while leading, but he still would have been leading. It was a gloomy day all around – for both Fangio and for myself. Both of us lost face. It remains one of my biggest disappointments in racing.'

Held on the last weekend in June, the Monza race was followed on the first weekend of July by the French Grand Prix at Reims. There, on the tenth anniversary of his first race in Europe, Fangio had personally entered a new version of the 250F Maserati to see how it would fare against the latest opposition. 'Maserati begged me to continue with them, even if only from time to time, to see how the 250F model would perform,' he said. 'Weight had been taken off it in various parts in order to compete with the lighter British cars. As always, the agreement was by word of mouth. I told my mechanics I would drive four races as long as the car went well.'

The Grand Prix picture had changed greatly, Juan well knew, for 1958. New regulations made the use of aviation-grade petrol mandatory and shortened championship Grand Prix races to 300 kilometres or two hours from the previous 500 kilometres or three hours. Both favoured the production of smaller, lighter cars which would be easier on their tyres. Also, the shorter races reduced the advantage of a durable driver of the Fangio class who could maintain high speed through a long contest. In addition, henceforth points would only be earned by a driver who finished in the car with which he started.

Juan Fangio had competed in the first race of this new era, the Argentine Grand Prix, on 19 January 1958. That it was won by Stirling Moss driving a spindly little 2-litre Cooper-Climax was seen as an aberration rather than the sign of the future it proved to be. Fangio drove a 1957-type works 250F entered by the Scuderia Sud Americana, a creation of his manager. With his habitual insouciance he had put it on pole and led the race – setting fastest lap – until a stop for tyres dropped him to fourth, where he finished behind Moss and two of the new Dino V6 Ferraris.

Fangio had left Indianapolis just in time to compete in the next championship GP at Monaco, where he was entered, but he did not appear. His rendezvous with the shorter, lighter *'Piccolo'* 1958 Maserati was at Reims instead. By then the Orsis had let it be known that Maserati was withdrawing from all factory racing activity. They did so to help get their financial house in order; in fact their works was under the protection of receivers while Maserati continued to service the cars of its customer racers.

The experienced Juan Manuel looked askance at

some of the features of the *Piccolo* 250F. The sight of orange Koni telescopic dampers, then new to Formula 1, did not please him. Also visible were Dunlop tyres instead of the Pirellis that had served him so well for so long. Invisible were the alterations to the Maserati six to make it run on petrol, which seemed less effective than the changes made by Vanwall and Ferrari. On this power circuit Fangio could qualify only eighth fastest.

Against all odds in the Grand Prix Fangio took the Maser to second place behind the ultimate winner, Hawthorn. But at mid-race the clutch pedal, drilled for lightness, broke off; an angry Juan handed it to Bertocchi at a quick pit stop. Shifting clutchless to the end he eked out a fourth-place finish. During this unsatisfying race Fangio had been thinking:

'Just before leaving my country in 1958 our family doctor told me: "Be careful, your father and mother are not so strong any more. After one of the recent races I found them very agitated." If I went on, I might only prove that I was stupid. The first race I won at Reims was in 1948, so it seemed right to quit there in 1958. I said to myself: "Here I started, here I finish."'

Like the 1948 French GP, in which a 56-year-old Tazio Nuvolari turned some of his final racing laps, the 1958 version had its watershed aspects. An era of prominence for Italy's drivers ended when Luigi Musso died after crashing. Among the newer names on the grid were Phil Hill, Carroll Shelby, Jo Bonnier, Jack Brabham, Wolfgang von Trips, Graham Hill and Cliff Allison.

Interested spectators were Dan Gurney and Bruce McLaren, who was competing in the Formula 2 race. Watching at the fast curve past the pits, McLaren said that 'Fangio was barrelling through on full noise with the 250F Maserati. He tweaked the tail out coming under the Dunlop Bridge and held the drift all the way through the curve.' Hawthorn was fast too, young Bruce observed, but 'he was working hard at the wheel and did not seem as neat as Fangio.' Even at 47 the Grand Master still had the power to educate.

'I had pursued and realised the great ambition of my life,' Fangio reflected in his book written with Giambertone. 'At first, a world title had been the limit of my hopes and my boldest dreams. Then I had to win a second one, after which it seemed only logical to try for a third. Then a fourth was added to the other three and the fifth confirmed that the others had not, perhaps, been due entirely to luck. It was then I saw that it was time for me to stop: my goal had been reached, and I had realised my ambition. Where was the incentive to continue and what value would yet another world title, if I could win it, have had for me? I had loved racing and I had devoted the best years of my life to it. Now I had reached the top and it was time for me to disappear from the scene. But do not think that it was easy.'

People kept it from being easy by making him offers to return to the track. 'They tried to tempt me back a few times,' Juan said. 'When British Petroleum invited me to Modena to shoot some driving scenes for the film *Tribute to Fangio*, the Maserati mechanics told me I'd broken the track record. They were trying to get me all enthusiastic about returning to racing. But very painfully I had managed to get racing out of my system.'

One of his first visits after making that decision was to Stuttgart to tell his old friends at Daimler-Benz. Over a cigarette (he was always a moderate smoker) he told Karl Kling, Rudy Uhlenhaut and press chief Artur 'Kai' Keser that his racing days were over. As a token of their respect and friendship they presented him and Beba with a gorgeous blue 300SL convertible. Alfred Neubauer personally handed over the keys. The car may now be seen in the Centro Technólogico-Cultural y Museo del Automovilismo Juan Manuel Fangio in Balcarce. Fangio became, and remained for life, the honorary president of Mercedes-Benz Argentina SA.

Unlike many drivers who retire, Juan Manuel Fangio did not avoid the tracks and the people of the sport he had pursued so rewardingly. His first public appearance after his decision was in the pits and paddock at Monza during practice for the Italian Grand Prix. He made the rounds with a quiet word and a handshake for adversaries old and new. Then he started the race, a ceremonial role he often performed later.

Nor did he remain a stranger to the cockpit. Two years after his retirement he stepped back into a 250F for the thrilling footage shot at the Modena Autodromo for BP's filmed tribute to his career. He's seen driving many of his championship cars in the film *Fangio* by Hugh Hudson and Giovanni Volpi, made in the early 1970s. In 1961 he joined Innes Ireland, Pedro Rodriguez, Masten Gregory, Denise McCluggage and others to hare around Connecticut's Lime Rock Park in Mini-Coopers.

His on-track demonstrations became as legendary as the man. Fans still talk about his quick recovery from a spin in the Alfetta before the pits at Laguna Seca. Bruce McLaren was at Cordoba in 1960 when Juan demonstrated some racers for his Argentine fans. 'Fangio tried his hand in a Formula 2 Porsche for a few laps,' said Bruce, 'then hopped into a 250F Maserati.' All went well until he spun it over a kerb and ended up with four bent wire wheels. Dan Gurney remembered the car bouncing about four feet in the air. McLaren: 'Fangio was lucky to escape injury and had our sympathy.'

Gurney was at Donington in Britain in 1979 when one of the awesome 580-horsepower 1937 Mercedes-Benz Grand Prix cars was wheeled out for Fangio to drive in a demonstration. 'I don't think he'd ever driven it before,' Dan said. 'He had an interpreter, and one of the mechanics he knew was explaining the gear selection. And the first time he came out of the last turn on to the pit straight he was on opposite lock. The Old Man did that four laps in a row, coming out of there on opposite lock. Everybody was so appreciative of the spirit of the guy.'

At Long Beach in 1976, in a classic-racer demonstration event before the first Grand Prix on that Californian street circuit, Dan Gurney 'raced' against Fangio's Mercedes-Benz W196. Instructed by owner Tom Wheatcroft not to 'hang about' in his Grand Prix BRM, Dan passed Fangio to 'win' the race. 'Afterward Fangio came over to me and mumbled something to me through his interpreter,' Dan recalled. 'The interpreter said to me, "Mr Fangio says, What's the idea of taking out an old man like that?"!' Senses of humour were still in fine working order on both sides.

Fangio was a passenger, not a driver, in a trip by car that made him far more famous in America than any of his racing successes. He was in Havana in February 1958 to compete with a Maserati in the sports-car Grand Prix of Cuba. Juan stayed with the Maserati team in the modest Lincoln Hotel. Carroll Shelby was also driving a Maserati:

'Right in the lobby, just before dinner on the night before the race, with Maserati people like Ugolini and Bertocchi standing there, and Moss, Trintignant and Behra on their way to the dining room, who walks in but this *Fideliste* in a soiled checkered shirt and pants that were just as dirty, wearing a Colt. Quick as the bat of an eyelash, this character disarmed the private detective assigned to Fangio by the Batista people and said something like, "Get up and follow me!" Fangio didn't really believe it at first. He suspected some kind of a legpull, another of those shenanigans that race drivers are always dreaming up. But he soon found out this was for real when a car whisked him off into the darkness.'

Fangio later had cause to thank his abductors. His luck was in again. Seven spectators were killed and 30 injured in the early laps of the race – which was stopped – while Fangio was being moved from house to house by the Fidel Castro rebels. After 26 hours he was released to the Argentine ambassador. Although he said he wouldn't recognise the men again, this wasn't quite true. 'Now one of the kidnappers is a Minister for Trade,' Juan Manuel said later. 'He sends me good luck telegrams.'

Among the thousands worried about the fate of the kidnapped five-time champion was Andreina 'Beba' Berruet Espinosa. Beba and her husband – who somewhat resembled Fangio – had lived not far from the driver in Balcarce. Divorce not being a possibility in Catholic Argentina, Juan and Beba had no option but to behave as man and wife. Theirs was a close and at times tempestuous relationship.

'In my life I had beside me a very strong woman,' Juan said of Beba. 'She was very jealous and did not want me to wander round too much. We were not married, but we spent 20 years together. Then one day we had a discussion and she said, "If you don't like being with me you may leave," so I left. When I finished with racing I finished with her. When a man and a woman start to lose mutual respect the time has come to finish.'

'He had no need at all to be married,' said close colleague Karl Kling of Fangio. 'He was married with many! Fangio loved and treasured women, but many. He was a man in demand. He was a charmer, even though he was a quite simple fellow – which I valued in him – but he was a charmer. He could be quite seductive to women, really nice. Women fancied him. Fangio was also quite often with Evita. He was often invited there for a coffee. What else went on, no one knows! There were always a few rumours about that, but ... everyone can think what he likes.'

Fangio was helped in these arrangements by his friends, one of them recalled: 'One time at the Nürburgring he brought this South American girl and all of a sudden his "wife" appeared, so we had to make the girl disappear.' A particular lady friend was the vivacious Belgian race and rally driver Gilberte Thirion. The friend: 'Once, even twice, in Belgium when he was with Thirion we had to take Gilberte away so that the "wife" didn't see her.'

We can only regret that Juan Fangio had no natural child. Andreina's son by her marriage, 'Cacho' Espinosa, bore a startling resemblance to Fangio but was not his son. Nevertheless Juan Manuel allowed him to use the 'Fangio' name – in the sense of a stage name – when they travelled to Europe and when the young man sought a career as a driver. Later, however, Fangio was unhappy about Espinosa's efforts in court (ultimately fruitless) to have the name made legally his.

'The first driver's career he helped promote,' wrote Stirling Moss, 'was Juan Manuel Bordeu, a young man he met by chance one day in a roadside restaurant, where a mutual friend introduced them. The youngster confided in Fangio that his ambition was to race in Europe, and to his astonishment the great man promptly invited him to a meeting in Buenos Aires to see what could be done.' Not without talent, Bordeu came to Europe after a successful South American career but an accident at Goodwood put paid to his hopes of a transition to Formula 1.

The next Fangio generation was well represented on the track by the son of his younger brother Toto Fangio. Even to his receding hairline the image of his namesake uncle, Juan Manuel Fangio II was so named in honour of Fangio's fourth world championship in 1956, the year of his nephew's birth. Driving for Dan Gurney's team for a dozen years, Juan II was twice winner of the Sebring 12 Hours and twice the drivers' champion in the American IMSA series. Although he retired from American racing in 1997 Juan II continued to compete in Argentina.

Juan Fangio I suffered a heart attack in 1970 that slowed him down for a while. Another episode in 1981 was a warning that his 'plumbing' needed attention; in 1982 his heart was given five bypasses. Plans made since the late 1970s to honour his career in Balcarce reached fruition in 1986 with the opening there of the exhibition-cum-collection that bears his name. 'I want a museum not for Fangio but for motor sports,' he said, 'to serve as examples for the young. To them it is dedicated.

'I hope that the objects on display will act as an incentive to greater enthusiasm,' Fangio said at the inauguration of his Centro Technólogico-Cultural, 'for a sport which doesn't seem to have a limit when it comes to speed, but must always be based on permanent values of manliness, bravery, mobility and honesty since in it life is risked, even though the triumph is that of the machine.'

In the mid-1990s Fangio's own machine began showing signs of wear. Frequent kidney dialysis was needed. On 15 July 1995 his condition worsened and he was moved to hospital in Buenos Aires. At 4.30 in the morning of 17 July, at the age of 84, he died. He was interred in the Balcarce cemetery the following day.

A full-page advertisement appeared in the Argentine papers. Above a small three-pointed star it showed a cloud-filled sky with rays of sun breaking through. 'If you hear thunder,' said its text, 'don't think that it's going to rain. It's Fangio testing a car.'

Peter Keen captures the playful side of Juan Manuel Fangio in four charming portraits taken at the time of the 1957 Italian Grand Prix. The five-times world champion is again beginning to weigh the idea of retirement.

More in hope than in expectation, Fangio tries a revised Maserati at Reims in 1958. Visibly struggling with its uncertain handling, Fangio decides during the race to retire as a driver: 'I did not relish the prospect of becoming an also-ran, and that is one of the main reasons why I was determined to retire when I had reached the peak.'

Fangio's long-held ambition to compete at Indianapolis leads to his entry there in 1958. Onlookers are amazed at the speeds he achieves in spite of his unorthodox line on the four-cornered oval. Although Juan elects not to qualify at Indianapolis, he qualifies for the subsequent 'Monzanapolis' race with a very quick time in the Offy-powered Dean Van Lines Special (overleaf). Thanks to engine problems he makes only a token appearance in its third heat.

29

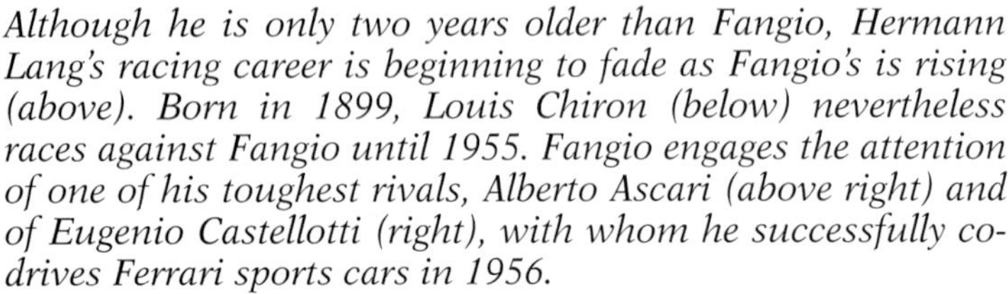

Although he is only two years older than Fangio, Hermann Lang's racing career is beginning to fade as Fangio's is rising (above). Born in 1899, Louis Chiron (below) nevertheless races against Fangio until 1955. Fangio engages the attention of one of his toughest rivals, Alberto Ascari (above right) and of Eugenio Castellotti (right), with whom he successfully co-drives Ferrari sports cars in 1956.

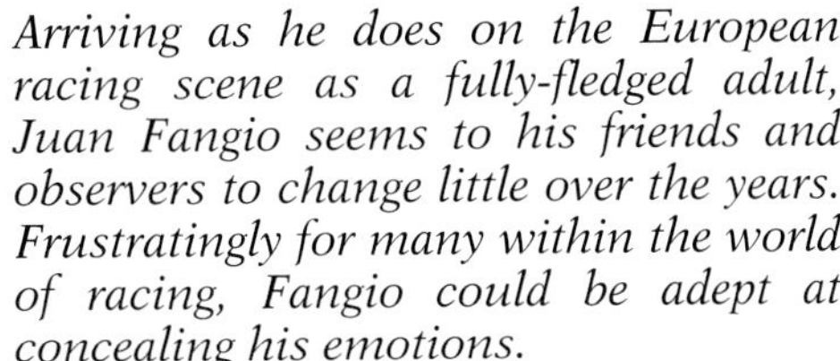

Arriving as he does on the European racing scene as a fully-fledged adult, Juan Fangio seems to his friends and observers to change little over the years. Frustratingly for many within the world of racing, Fangio could be adept at concealing his emotions.

That populist Argentine leader Juan Perón values the contributions Fangio makes to his country is never in doubt (above left and right). But unlike others the canny Fangio does not fall under the Perón spell. With Luigi Fagioli and Nino Farina he meets Britain's King George VI at Silverstone in 1950 (below left). He is on hand when Sweden's Prince Bertil, a great car enthusiast, visits Daimler-Benz in Stuttgart (below right).

Well appreciated by his employers, Fangio receives a stick pin from Fritz Nallinger of Daimler-Benz in 1955 and an Alfetta steering wheel from Alfa Romeo's Giuseppe Luraghi in 1965 (above right). Guidotti points out its inscribed dedication. Fangio meets Cuba's dictator Battista in 1958 (below left) and, with Neubauer, French driver René Thomas (below right), winner of the 1914 Indianapolis 500-mile race.

The limelight beckons for racing drivers in the Fifties, especially for Fangio. Clockwise from top left he is filmed for the news at Monza in 1954, with mechanic Weber behind him, is interviewed for the crowd before the 1952 Mille Miglia in Brescia, speaks to the grandstands at the 1951 Modena Grand Prix, and joins Kling, Neubauer and a moderator for television in 1954.

Photos of particular interest to the creators of this book include one by the author showing Fangio inspecting the engine of the Maserati he demonstrates at Thompson Raceway in March 1954, and an attractive view of the champion and Beba, at the end of his Mercedes-Benz career, in which Rudy Mailander stands behind the lady.

The fair sex reciprocate Fangio's manifest interest in them. He was, in Karl Kling's words, 'a charmer'. He poses with a comely ragazza *after the 1954 Italian Grand Prix, attracts the attention of mantilla-clad ladies of Spain in Barcelona in the same year, and enjoys the enthusiastic welcome of a largely feminine crowd on a Daimler-Benz works visit at the end of that season. And if his companion Beba is 'a very strong woman', as Fangio says, she could well be getting on his nerves during the pre-practice for Reims in 1954.*

Beba could not have been pleased with the friendship that developed between Fangio and Belgian racer Gilberte Thirion, especially in the 1951 season. In her flowered dress Thirion is conspicuous with Fangio and Zanardi after his victory in the 1951 French Grand Prix. Gilberte is on hand as well at the Spanish Grand Prix with cardigan over her shoulders. At Monza that year she waits impatiently for Fangio to finish his conversation with Giovanni Lurani.

The off-duty Fangio is seen driving in retirement, at the wheel of a Chevrolet, selecting his reading for a train trip to Syracuse in Sicily in the company of (left) fellow Argentine Alejandro de Tomaso and Milan Ferrari dealer Gastone Crepaldi, in a game of cards with Moss and Kling with a gleeful Neubauer kibitzing, and in Milan with Beba and one of the Sojit brothers. And if in the sunset of his years as a racing driver he drives off with Beba in a spectacular 300SL Roadster, who would dare deny him that privilege?

S-EV 889

al amigo Karl Ludvigsen

J M Fangio

Annotated bibliography

Beaumont, Charles and Nolan, William F. *Omnibus of Speed* (G. P. Putnam's Sons, New York, 1958). 480pp, many line drawings

This is an anthology with no photographs, and is split into four sections on general motorsports, men, machines and arenas. All the pieces, written by individual authors, are taken from earlier publications. The chapter on Fangio, titled 'Wary Old Daredevil', is written by Marshall Smith and includes an interesting footnote on how Fangio survived a potentially fatal road accident in Italy driving a Lancia.

Brawner, Clint and Scalzo, Joe *Indy 500 Mechanic* (Chilton Book Company, Pennsylvania, 1975). 194pp, 30 photographs

The contents are largely what you would expect from the title, but the narrative also includes the Race of Two Worlds, better known these days as Monzanapolis, run in 1957 and 1958. Fangio drove in the 1958 event and also visited Indy that year, and Brawner prepared Fangio's car at Monza.

Chuhran, John 'The Maestro' (*The Star*, September/October 1995). 7pp, 4 photographs

Article written after Fangio's death in 1995 celebrating his career and persona.

Cooper, John with Bentley, John *The Grand Prix Carpet-Baggers* (Doubleday & Company Inc, New York, 1977). 230pp, 48 photographs

Written in co-operation with veteran British journalist then resident in America, John Bentley, this predates the better-known Nye work by three years. It is more personal and includes the meeting Cooper had with the reclusive and eccentric Howard Hughes. Fangio of course drove the prototype Cooper Bristol at Goodwood in 1952, notable for the fact, as related by John Cooper, that Fangio was paid no starting money!

Fangio, Juan Manuel with Carozzo, Roberto *Fangio, My Racing Life* (Patrick Stephens Limited, 1990). 367pp, 87 photographs

Actually written in 1986, its preface by Fangio states that 'I have never before taken any direct part in any book written about me.' This is the most detailed of all the Fangio works, albeit in a somewhat disorderly fashion, and edited by Denis Jenkinson. However, it is packed with information and also reveals how professional and thoughtful JMF was about his driving (unlike some of his contemporaries) and how humble were his origins.

Fangio, Juan Manuel 'Complete Retirement' (*Autosport*, 21 November 1958). 2½pp, 5 photographs

JMF discussing his retirement in *Autosport* magazine and facing the reality of the passing years, which he had overcome better than anyone.

Frère, Paul *Sports Car and Competition Driving* (Robert Bentley Inc, 1963). 144pp, 58 photographs

Similar but more accessible tome on how to drive quickly than the more famous Taruffi book. Frère is always erudite and the result is a fascinating insight into the period, which features various driver comments including Fangio's blunt advice to Claes on how to go faster – 'Less brakes and more accelerator'.

Giambertone, Marcello *Fangio* (Louvain Landsborough, 1963). 222pp, 8 photographs

Paperback version of the 1961 Temple Press hardback, supposedly written in collaboration with Fangio, which he later disowned. Giambertone was his manager, another thing that Ferrari held against Fangio, the great and autocratic Enzo preferring to dictate terms directly to his drivers.

Grant, Gregor 'The Champion of Champions' (*Autosport*, 1 August 1958). 3pp, 4 photographs

Brief appraisal of Fangio's career after his retirement by the founder of *Autosport*, Gregor Grant.

Hansen, Ronald and Kirbus, Federico B. *The Life Story of Juan Manuel Fangio* (Edita SA, Lausanne, 1956). 78pp, 19 photographs

Despite the title, this work actually covers up to the start of the 1956 season. Nevertheless it is worthy of mention and concise. The publisher is best remembered for the original *Automobile Year* annuals.

Heglar, Mary Schnall *The Grand Prix Champions* (Bond Parkhurst Books, 1973). 234pp, 102 photographs

A pot-pourri of World Champions from 1950 to 1972, which gives 16 pages to Fangio's life.

Herrmann, Hans *Ein Leben für den Rennsport* (Motorbuch-Verlag, Stuttgart, 1998). 248pp, hundreds of photographs, German text

Although best remembered for his BRM crash at Avus, Porsche drives in the 1960s and finally retiring after winning Le Mans in 1970, Herrmann was one of the original Mercedes W196 drivers along with Fangio, Kling and Lang. His Silver Arrows career ended against a balustrade at Monaco in 1955, an accident that he was lucky to survive. This book is worth buying for the photographs even if you don't read German.

Huet, Christian *Gordini – Un Sorcier Une Equipe* (Editions Christian Huet, 1984). 485pp, hundreds of photographs, French text

Many forget or perhaps are unaware that Fangio raced Gordinis on nine occasions, including Le Mans 1950. This is a fabulous book with many unfamiliar photos. Fangio has written an affectionate foreword.

Jenkinson, Denis 'Fangio' (*Autocourse*, 1995–1996). 272pp, hundreds of colour photographs

DSJ reminiscing about the deceased Fangio in a feature that has a rarely-seen colour shot of JMF talking to Peter Collins.

Jenkinson, Denis *Fangio* (W. W. Norton Inc, 1973). 144pp, 114 b/w and 18 colour photographs

Edited as distinct from written by 'Jenks', this is a well-captioned photo book based on the Hugh Hudson film, let down by poor reproduction and typical 1970s design. It is also one of the few Fangio books that makes it clear that JMF was not married to his long-time partner Donna Andreina, nicknamed 'Beba', who was normally referred to as his wife.

Jenkinson, Denis *Jenks – A Passion for Motor Sport* (Motor Racing Publications Limited, 1997). 224pp, 138 photographs

This collection of the best of 'Jenks' over the years includes several pages on Fangio. It is otherwise a very interesting, if at times subjective, read and includes appreciations from Nye, Boddy, Roebuck *et al.*

McLaren, Bruce *From the Cockpit* (Frederick Muller Limited, 1964). 278pp, 24 photographs

Reading this simple story of a boy who fought back from a crippling childhood disease to become the youngest-ever Grand Prix winner and the founder of one of the greatest F1 teams ever, it is impossible to relate the man to the latter-day high-tech fiefdom of Ron Dennis. McLaren saw Fangio race at Reims in 1958 and interestingly mentions how at Cordoba in 1960 Fangio drove an F2 Porsche, then a 250F Maserati, which he spun.

Merlin, Olivier *Fangio, Racing Driver* (Robert Bentley Inc, 1961). Originally published in Belgium under the title of *Fangio – Pilote de Course* by Desclee de Brouwer in 1959. 216pp, 51 photographs

A good selection of pictures, and covers his entire racing career, suffering only from the rather flowery prose typical of translated works.

Molter, Günther *Juan Manuel Fangio, World Champion* (G. T. Foulis, 1956). Translated by Charles Meisl. 184pp, 62 photographs

This is a good book that rather oddly stops after the 1955 British Grand Prix. It also offers a selection of pictures not too often seen elsewhere. Later Molter became the Mercedes-Benz press chief.

Molter, Günther *Pursuit of Victory – The Story of a Racing Driver* (The Bodley Head, 1956). First published by Blüchert-Verlag, Stuttgart, 1954. 192pp, 93 photographs

Typical period biography but with more photos than normal, and translated from the German by Peter Myers, this is the story of Karl Kling, a man who came too late on the scene thanks to the war. Like all his contemporaries he suffered from having the ultimate team-mate (Fangio) at Mercedes-Benz. It finishes with a chapter written by his long-suffering wife, noting their gypsy-like existence during 'The Season'. Kling has never received the recognition he deserves.

Moss, Stirling with Nye, Doug in association with Mercedes-Benz *Fangio, A Pirelli Album* (Pavilion Books, 1991). 168pp, 140 b/w and 58 colour photographs

Landscape-format book that is a homage to Fangio with many period black and white images of varying quality interspersed with contemporary and period colour. There are plenty of anecdotes and quotes with comment from Moss. Of interest in these paranoid, drug-obsessed times are the 'Dynavis' pills that Fangio used to alleviate his great thirst in long races. Moss (who used them once only for the 1955 Mille Miglia, which he won) had his dentist father analyse them. He discovered an unidentifiable ingredient. They were made in Switzerland and marketed commercially.

Nixon, Chris 'Enzo's Right-Hand Man' (*Motorsport*, November 1998). 3pp, 8 photographs

Article on Romolo Tavoni and his travails as Ferrari team manager in the 1950s. Once again Ferrari's hostility to Fangio surfaces. Tavoni revealed that the mercurial Hawthorn was his favourite driver, and also one of the few to stand up to Enzo.

Nixon, Chris *Mon Ami Mate – The Bright Brief Lives of Mike Hawthorn and Peter Collins* (Transport Bookman, 1991). 377pp, many hundreds of photographs

As with Moss, so with Fangio, and any driver of the period had to beat one or the other, or – worse still – both. It is a wonder that anybody managed it at all. Nixon gives Fangio a whole chapter as he was central to the careers of both Hawthorn and Collins.

Nye, Doug with Rudd, Tony *BRM, Volume One* (Motor Racing Publications, 1994). 432pp, hundreds of b/w and colour photographs

Nye's magnum opus on the Bourne constructors and a fascinating addition to Rudd's autobiography. Fangio's genius is highlighted in his driving of the infamous V16.

Nye, Doug *Great Racing Drivers* (Hamlyn Publishing Group, 1977). 156pp, 113 b/w and 12 colour photographs

Almost a potboiler by Nye's standards, it nevertheless features over 50 drivers, including of course Fangio, with each given a brief biography.

Rayner, Richard 'Fangio, Still Racing After All These Years' (*Telegraph Magazine*, 13 April 1991). 7pp, 10 b/w and 2 colour photographs.

Interview with Fangio based on the Moss/Nye photobiography *Fangio* of that year.

Riedner, Michael *Mercedes-Benz W196, Last of the Silver Arrows* (Haynes Publishing, 1990). First published in 1986 in German by Motorbuch-Verlag, Stuttgart. 325pp, hundreds of photographs

A very thorough book on the car, the drivers, team personnel, the races and inevitably some historical background. Also includes six pages on the 300SLR plus a chapter on the 1955 Le Mans tragedy, which partly blames Mike Hawthorn.

Roebuck, Nigel *Grand Prix Greats* (Patrick Stephens Limited, 1986). 216pp, 149 photographs and 25 portrait paintings

The author chose 25 drivers for his book, which of course included Fangio, whom he met at Monaco in 1971. Written in his usual authoritative and incisive style, this captures the essence of the great man well.

Rudd, Tony *It Was Fun* (Patrick Stephens Limited, 1993). 352pp, 83 photographs

Tony Rudd's extraordinary career spanned over 50 years from his family connection with HRH Prince Chula Chakrabongse, patron of 'B. Bira', to his last involvement with Lotus. In between he was the technical brains of BRM, even getting the temperamental V16 to run properly on occasion. Fangio of course drove it better than anyone else and loved the power. This is a fascinating book.

Schuler, Steve *Fangio – Auto Racing Analysis 1998*

A fully tabulated and annotated list of Fangio's racing career compiled for this book project, giving venue, date, cars driven, results and/or reasons for retirement. A superb source of information that is highly recommended.

Sculati, Eraldo *Ferrari 1956* (Scuderia Ferrari Editions, 1956). 89pp, 169 photographs, Italian text

Softback Ferrari yearbook memorable for the moving letter addressed to the recently deceased Dino Ferrari by his father. It covers Ferrari activities and celebrity customers for the 1956 season with an alphabetical section of drivers and associated personnel that is an excellent source for putting lesser-known names to faces. Tellingly the entry for Fangio is qualified by the comment that his world championship was made possible by the other Ferrari drivers and the efforts of the Scuderia Ferrari team. No love lost here.

Stern, Michael 'El Chueco' (*Cars*, June 1953). 5pp, 7 photographs

Feature in the long-defunct American magazine; set early in his European career, it describes how popular Fangio was even then.

Walkerley, Rodney 'Passing of an Epoch' (*Autosport*, 25 November–20 January 1961). 39pp, 58 photographs

A succinct and well-written precis of the 1954–1960 2.5-litre F1 era, with various tabulated results and data. It highlights Fangio's dominance of four of the Formula's seven years.

Wilkins, Gordon 'Juan Manuel Fangio' (*Auto Age*, 1956). 6pp, 14 b/w and 2 colour photographs

A typical piece written at the end of 1955 after Fangio's third world championship, which gives a brief outline of the Argentine's career to date.

Wilkins, Gordon 'With Fangio' (*Motor Trend*, June 1958). 2pp, no photographs

Article in a period American journal with Fangio telling renowned British journalist Gordon Wilkins about his 1957 German Grand Prix victory over lunch at the RAC Club in London.

Photograph credits

Archivio Alfa Romeo: P60 upper left, P67, P77, P92 upper, P93 upper right, P192 lower left, P193 upper right.

Dr Vicente Alvarez: P45 upper left.

Andre Van Bever: P152.

Bernard Cahier: Frontispiece, P93 lower right, P103, P122 upper, P126 right, P138, P148 upper left & right, lower right, P150–151, P156, P169 lower, P170 upper right, P171 lower, P172 upper & lower, P173 upper, P176 upper & lower, P186 lower, P193 lower left, rear endpaper.

Peter Coltrin Archive: P186 upper, P198 upper left.

Lawrence Crane: P101 lower.

Daimler-Benz Archive: P9, P10, P18, P19 lower left & right, P26–27, P28, P29 upper, P109 lower, P113–114, P121, P122 lower, P123, P125, P126 upper left & centre, centre left, P128–129 lower, P130, P134 upper, P135 lower, P136 upper & lower left, lower right, P137 upper left & right, lower right, P190 upper left & right, lower right, P191 upper right, lower left, centre & right, P192 upper & lower right, P193 upper left & lower right, P194 upper left & lower right, P195 right, P196, P198 lower right, P199.

Yves Debraine: P99 upper, P108 lower.

Edward Eves from Ludvigsen Library: P45 upper right.

Archivio Ferrari: P45 lower right, P48–49, P60, P198 middle left & right.

Fundacion Museo del Automovilismo 'Juan Manuel Fangio': P21, P22–23, P24–25, P30 lower, P31 lower.

Guy Griffiths: P60 lower left, P88 upper, P98 upper, P101 upper, P108 upper.

Peter Keen from Ludvigsen Library: P165 upper right & lower right, P173 lower, P174–175, P185, P198 lower left.

The Klemantaski Collection: P100, P102, P104/105.

LAT Photographic: P97, P98 lower, P99 lower, P106–107, P110–111, P112.

Éditions Maurice Louche: P44 lower right, P25–26.

Karl Ludvigsen from Ludvigsen Library: P170 lower, P171 upper.

Ludvigsen Library: P19 upper left, P29 lower, P30–31 upper, P32, P39, P40–41, P42–43, P45 lower left, P46–47, P52, P61, P62–63, P66 upper & lower right, P73 lower, P76 centre, P87 left, P88 lower, P89, P90–91, P109 upper, P126 centre middle, lower left & middle, P135 upper, P137 lower left, P145, P146–147, P148 lower left, P149, P169 upper, P177, P187, P188–189, P195 left, P197 upper left, P200.

Rodolfo Mailander from Ludvigsen Library: front endpaper, P44 lower left, upper left & right, P59, P60 upper & lower right, P64–65, P66 upper & lower left, P68–69, P70–71, P72, P73 upper, P74–75, P76 upper & lower, P78, P85, P86, P87 right, P92 lower, P93 upper & lower left, P94, P95 upper, P96, P124, P126 middle right & lower right, P127, P128–129 upper, P131, P132–133, P134 lower, P136 upper right, P165 upper left, P178, P190 lower left, P191 upper left & centre, P194 lower left & upper right, P197 lower left, upper & lower right.

Archivio Maserati: P95 left & right, P163, P164, P165 lower left, P166–167, P168, P170 left, P192 upper left, P198 upper right.

James Sitz: P155.

Tony Watson: P17.

Index

CARS INDEX